Unwrapped success

Leveraging digital marketing strategies for holiday season success

By

Laurel M. West

Table of contents

Introduction

Welcome to the advanced wonderland of occasional advertising! As the happy season draws near, organizations are preparing for the joyful dance of catching crowd consideration, spreading cheer, and driving accomplishment through key computerized showcasing. In this guide, we'll take you on a journey to discover how to use digital marketing strategies to succeed this holiday season. From exploring the clamoring on the web scene to making stunning efforts that stick out, go along with us as we open up the critical bits of knowledge and strategies that will make your image sparkle in the midst of the occasion. Prepare to enhance your presence, associate with your crowd, and sway the opposition in this happy computerized experience!

As the Christmas season draws near, the computerized domain changes into a clamoring commercial center enhanced with merry missions and energetic advancements. In the midst of the gleaming lights and cheerful tunes, organizations set out on a mission to tackle the force of computerized marketing for occasional victory. In this article, we explore the scene of utilizing computerized showcasing systems for Christmas season achievement. From stunning virtual entertainment exhibitions to enrapturing email crusades, we dive into the workmanship and study of catching the hearts and wallets of purchasers during this happy time. Go along with us on this computerized sled ride as we open up the key to making a full internet-based presence, spreading seasonal joy, and guaranteeing your image sparkles brilliantly all through the season.

A comprehensive structure for a guide that discusses various aspects of utilizing digital marketing strategies during the holiday season is provided by this outline. Each segment can be extended with pertinent bits of knowledge, models, and significant hints to make a nitty-gritty and educational asset for organizations.

The Christmas season isn't just a period of festivity; it is additionally a superb chance for organizations to have a tremendous effect in the computerized circle. Utilizing computerized promotion systems during this bubbly period includes an insightful mix of innovativeness, key preparation, and crowd commitment. In this extensive aide, we'll investigate key components of effective occasion advertising efforts, including virtual entertainment procedures that enhance brand perceivability, email promoting strategies that reverberate with bubbly soul, and site improvement methods that guarantee your contributions are found in the midst of the advanced occasion buzz. Whether you're a carefully prepared advertiser or exploring the occasion to showcase a scene interestingly, this guide is intended to furnish you with the bits of knowledge and techniques expected to make your image stick out, interface with your crowd, and sway the opposition during this otherworldly season. Prepare to unlock the full potential of digital marketing for a prosperous and joyful holiday season.

Overview of the Significance of Holiday Season for Businesses

The Christmas season holds massive importance for organizations across different enterprises, filling in as a urgent time that can fundamentally affect their prosperity and in general execution. Here is an outline of the key perspectives featuring the significance of the Christmas season for organizations:

1. Top Shopping Period: The Christmas season, commonly beginning around Thanksgiving and reaching out through the New Year, points a pinnacle period for customer spending.

People participate in present purchasing, bubbly beautifications, and generally expanded retail movement.

2. Boost in Revenue: Organizations frequently experience a significant lift in income during the Christmas season. The flood in buyer spending presents a chance for expanded deals, making it a crucial time for accomplishing monetary objectives.

3. Vital Advertising Open doors: The Christmas season gives an essential window to organizations to send off designated promoting efforts. Bubbly advancements, extraordinary offers, and inventive promoting drives catch the consideration of customers effectively looking for occasion related items and administrations.

4. Brand Perceivability and Acknowledgment: Compelling occasion showcasing adds to elevated brand perceivability and acknowledgment. Organizations that effectively adjust their items or administrations to the happy soul can have an enduring effect on shoppers, cultivating brand unwaveringness.

5. Client Obtaining and Maintenance: The flood of occasion customers sets out open doors for organizations to gain new clients. Also, decisively arranged advancements and superb client encounters during this period add to client maintenance and devotion.

6. Web based business Flood: E-commerce activities significantly increase during the holiday season as a result of the rise of online shopping. Organizations with a solid web-based presence can take advantage of this computerized market and profit by the developing pattern of online Christmas shopping.

7. Possibility of Seasonal Offers: Occasional or occasion themed items and administrations gain unmistakable quality during this

time. Organizations can present restricted time contributions, selective arrangements, and happy varieties to draw in clients looking for extraordinary and celebratory encounters.

8. Local area Commitment: The Christmas season presents an optimal chance for organizations to draw in with their nearby networks. A brand's reputation can be improved by participating in holiday events, donating to charitable causes, and fostering a sense of community involvement.

9. End-of-year sales targets: For some organizations, the Christmas season denotes the last stretch in accomplishing yearly deals objectives. Effectively profiting by the merry soul permits organizations to meet or surpass their year-end targets.

10. Social Importance: Special times of year hold social importance, and organizations that adjust their advertising endeavors to these social components can reverberate all the more profoundly with their interest group. Marketing campaigns are more successful when they are based on an understanding of and respect for cultural traditions.

Basically, the Christmas season isn't just a period of festivity yet additionally a basic period for organizations to decisively situate themselves, interface with customers, and accomplish both present moment and long-haul goals. It is a one-of-a-kind chance for businesses to spread joy, build relationships, and thrive in a lively and festive market.

Importance of Digital Marketing in Capturing Seasonal Opportunities

Computerized showcasing assumes a vital role in catching occasional open doors, particularly during huge periods like the

Christmas season. Here are key reasons for the significance of computerized promotion in this unique circumstance:

1. Activity Online Is Up: During the Christmas season, there's a significant expansion in web-based exercises, including shopping, exploration, and virtual entertainment. Computerized promotion empowers organizations to reach and interface with shoppers in the spaces where they spend a lot of their time.

2. Focused on and Customized Missions: Advanced promotion permits organizations to make focused on and customized crusades custom-made to explicit crowd sections. This accuracy guarantees that limited-time endeavors are bound to reverberate with buyers looking for occasional items or services.

3. Continuous Flexibility: Campaigns can be adjusted in real time using digital marketing channels based on consumer habits and market trends. Organizations can rapidly change methodologies to profit by opening doors or addressing unforeseen difficulties during the high-speed Christmas season.

4. Worldwide Reach: Computerized showcasing rises above geological limits, empowering organizations to contact a worldwide crowd. This is especially favorable during the Christmas season, when individuals all over the planet are effectively taking part in bubbly exercises and festivities.

5. Virtual Entertainment Commitment: Web-based entertainment stages become dynamic centers of movement during special times of the year. Computerized showcasing on friendly channels permits organizations to draw in with their crowd through outwardly engaging substance, challenges, and advancements, encouraging a feeling of local area and energy.

6. Web-based business mix: The Christmas season sees a flood in web-based shopping. Digital marketing makes it easier for businesses to show off their products, run promotions, and increase sales directly through digital channels because it allows for seamless integration with e-commerce platforms.

7. Information Investigation and Experiences: Advanced showcasing devices provide powerful investigation and experiences. Organizations can use information to comprehend purchaser conduct, track crusade execution, and pursue information-driven choices to improve their systems for improved results.

8. Email Advertising Adequacy: Email showcasing stays an amazing asset for catching occasional open doors. Organizations can utilize email missions to share exceptional offers, feature merry items, and support client connections during the Christmas season.

9. Visibility in Search Engines: Improving computerized content for web indexes guarantees organizations are discoverable when buyers effectively look for occasional items or services. Search engine optimization methodologies upgrade perceivability and increase the possibilities of drawing in expected clients.

10. Practical Missions: Computerized showcasing frequently offers practical options in contrast to customary promotion. Without the constraints of traditional advertising costs, businesses can effectively allocate budgets and reach a larger audience.

11. Communication on time: Computerized advertising empowers organizations to convey convenient data about advancements, limits, and unique occasions. Fast and effective

correspondence is fundamental during the fleeting chances of the Christmas season.

In synopsis, the significance of advanced promotion in catching occasional open doors lies in its capacity to associate organizations with their ideal interest group continuously, across borders, and through customized and drawn-in crusades. Digital channels give you the flexibility and reach you need to get the most out of the competitive and dynamic holiday market.

Chapter 1: Understanding Holiday Shopping Trends

Understanding Christmas shopping patterns is critical for organizations to adjust their techniques to buyers ways of behaving and inclinations during this happy season. Here are key bits of knowledge about Christmas shopping patterns:

1. Early Purchases: A critical pattern is the ascent of early seasonal shopping. Buyers begin exploring and making purchases a long time before conventional shopping tops, exploiting early advancements and limits.

2. Dominance Online: Online shopping is becoming increasingly popular. Internet business stages and portable applications have become favored channels for comfort, assortment, and the capacity to effectively think about costs.

3. Portable Shopping: Cell phones assume a focal point in Christmas shopping. Shoppers use cell phones for item research, value correlation, and making purchases. For a smooth shopping experience, websites and apps must be mobile-friendly.

4. Research-Arranged Customers: Before making a purchase decision, consumers conduct extensive product research. Online

recommendations, ratings, and reviews have a significant impact on decisions, highlighting the significance of managing one's reputation online.

5. Multi-Channel Shopping: Customers frequently participate in multi-channel shopping, consolidating on the web and having disconnected encounters. They might explore on the web yet make buys come up or the other way around, stressing the requirement for an incorporated retail approach.

6. Ethical and sustainable shopping: There is a developing pattern toward practical and moral shopping. Customers look for items with eco-accommodating bundling, moral obtaining, and a pledge to social obligation.

7. Personalization Assumptions: Purchasers value customized shopping encounters. Organizations that tailor suggestions, advancements, and correspondence in light of individual inclinations will generally stand apart during the Christmas season.

8. Experiences and Gift Cards: Gift vouchers and experiential gifts gain prominence. Purchasers value the adaptability and individuality of present cards, while encounters, for example, spa medicines or travel, are viewed as paramount options in contrast to conventional gifts.

9. Online Entertainment Impact: Online entertainment stages fundamentally impact shopping choices. Buyers find items through web-based entertainment channels, and forces to be reckoned with assume an essential part in molding inclinations and patterns.

10. Streak Deals and Restricted Time Offers: Restricted time advancements and glimmer deals make it necessary to keep

moving. Customers are bound to make purchases when they feel they are getting selective arrangements that are time-delicate.

11. Preferences for Contactless Payments: The inclination for contactless installments and advanced wallets keeps on rising. Giving secure and helpful computerized installment choices improves the general shopping experience.

12. Curbside Pickup and Impromptu Conveyance: The interest in helpful satisfaction choices like curbside pickup and impromptu conveyance has expanded. Buyers value the adaptability and speed these administrations offer, particularly during the rush.

13. Neighborhood and independent companies Backing: The importance of supporting local businesses is growing. Buyers effectively search out novel items from neighborhood retailers and value the customized administration they offer.

14. During longer shopping seasons: The Christmas shopping season has reached out past conventional dates. The biggest shopping day of the year and the Monday following Thanksgiving stay huge, yet organizations that broaden advancements all through the season can catch purchaser interest over a more extended period.

14. During longer shopping seasons: The Christmas shopping season has reached out past conventional dates. The biggest shopping day of the year and the Monday following Thanksgiving stay huge, yet organizations that broaden advancements all through the season can catch purchaser interest over a more extended period.

Understanding these seasonal shopping patterns permits organizations to tailor their promotion, stock, and client care systems to meet the advancing assumptions for purchasers during this merry period. It's fundamental for organizations to remain dexterous and adjust their methodologies in light of these patterns to boost their prosperity during the Christmas season.

Researching and Analyzing Consumer Behavior

Investigating and breaking down purchaser conduct is a basic part of creating powerful promotion methodologies. Understanding shoppers' thought process, simply decide, and communicate with items or administrations gives significant experiences that organizations can use to improve their contributions and commitment. Here is a breakdown of the interaction:

1. Market Study:
   Purpose: Learn about the market as a whole and who your ideal customers are.
   Methods: interviews, surveys, focus groups, and data analysis.
   Insights: socioeconomics, inclinations, and general customer feeling.

2. Analytics Online:
   Purpose: Examine computerized collaborations and conduct.
   Methods: site investigation, web-based entertainment bits of knowledge, and internet-following devices.
   Insights: online visits, navigate rates, skip rates, and client socioeconomics.

3. Reviews and Surveys:
   Purpose: Assemble explicit data straightforwardly from shoppers.
   Methods: online overviews, email surveys, or in-person meetings.

Insights: preferences, opinions, and feedback regarding products or services.

4. Analysis of Purchase History:
   Purpose: Comprehend past purchasing behaviors and inclinations.
   Methods: Investigate deals and buy chronicles.
   Insights: well-known items, normal request values, and recurrence of buys.

5. Web-based Entertainment Tuning in:
   Purpose: Screen and examine discussions via web-based entertainment stages.
   Methods: Tools for monitoring social media and sentiment analysis
   Insights: brand notices, feels, and arising patterns

6. Conduct financial matters:
   Purpose: Investigate the psychological factors that influence consumer choices.
   Methods: social examinations, reviews, and observational exploration.
   Insights: Grasping how feelings, predispositions, and social impacts influence purchasing conduct.

7. Center Gatherings:
   Purpose: Assemble subjective information and bits of knowledge from a different gathering of members.
   Methods: Directed bunch conversations with chosen members.
   Insights: an in-depth comprehension of attitudes, beliefs, and perceptions.

8. Psychographic Profiling:
   Purpose: Portion buyers in view of their way of life, values, and interests.
   Methods: overviews, meetings, and examination of social and online ways of behaving.
   Insights: Grasping inspirations and psychographic profiles of various shopper portions.

9. Client   Excursion   Planning:
   Purpose: Imagine and comprehend the stages clients go through while cooperating with an item or administration.
   Methods: information examination, client meetings, and criticism   assortment.
   Insights: recognizing touchpoints, trouble spots, and regions for development in the client venture.

10. The   A/B   Test:
    Purpose: Explore different avenues regarding varieties in promoting procedures to distinguish the best methodologies.
    Methods: experimenting with various ad, email, and website   layouts.
    Insights: quantitative information on which varieties perform better with the interest group.

Neuro-marketing:
Purpose: Grasp shopper reactions at a neurological level.
Methods: cerebrum imaging, eye following, and physiological estimations.
Insights: Uncover subliminal responses, close-to-home

reactions, and consideration levels during the dynamic interaction.

Investigating shopper conduct is a continuous interaction that requires a blend of quantitative and subjective examination strategies. Organizations can utilize these bits of knowledge to tailor their promoting messages, further develop client encounters, and make items or administrations that resonate with their main interest group. Routinely refreshing and refining techniques in light of advancing customer conduct guarantees pertinence and viability in the unique market scene.

Identifying Key Trends in E-commerce and Retail

A few key patterns are forming the scene of web-based business and retail, mirroring the developing inclinations and ways of behaving of customers. Here are a few prominent patterns in these areas:

1. Omnichannel Retail:
Description: Consistent reconciliation of on-the-web and disconnected retail encounters.
Impact: Buyers anticipate a durable encounter across various channels, including actual stores, sites, and portable applications.

2. Versatile Shopping Predominance:
Description: Expanding dependence on cell phones for web-based shopping.
Impact: Internet business stages should focus on versatile enhancement, responsiveness, and portable installment choices.

3. Social Trade:
Description: Joining of shopping highlights into virtual entertainment stages.

Impact: A seamless shopping experience is made possible by consumers' direct product discovery and purchase within social apps.

4. Personalization and simulated intelligence:
Description: Utilization of man-made brainpower for customized shopping encounters.
Impact: Computer-based intelligence-driven item proposals, customized promotion messages, and chatbots upgrade client commitment and fulfillment.

5. Manageable and Moral Practices:
Description: escalating demand from customers for goods sourced sustainably and ethically.
Impact: Organizations taking on eco-accommodating practices and straightforward stock chains gain favor among naturally cognizant customers.

6. Expanded Reality (AR) and Augmented Reality (VR):
Description: Integration of augmented reality and virtual reality for immersive shopping experiences
Impact: Virtual attempt-Ons, 360-degree item perspectives, and AR-empowered shopping improve online client commitment.

7. Voice Business:
Description: shopping online with voice-activated devices.
Impact: Voice search and voice-initiated shopping colleagues impact buying choices, expecting organizations to upgrade to voice search.

8. Models that rely on subscriptions:
Description: Expanding ubiquity of membership administrations for items.
Impact: Membership boxes, repeating conveyances, and

enrollment models give accommodation and assemble client unwaveringness.

9. Contactless Installments:
Description: Developing an inclination for contactless and advanced installment techniques.
Impact: expanded reception of advanced wallets, portable installment applications, and contactless card exchanges for protected and effective exchanges.

10. Purchase Currently, Pay Later (BNPL):
Description: the development of options for installment payments for online purchases.
Impact: The BNPL administration appeals to thrifty buyers, giving them adaptability in installments.

11. Environmental and social responsibility:
Description: Accentuation on corporate social obligation (CSR) and moral strategic approaches.
Impact: Purchasers are bound to help marks that line up with their qualities, prompting expanded brand devotion.

12. Live Trade:
Description: Continuous, intuitive shopping encounters through live video in real time.
Impact: Brands associate with purchasers progressively, displaying items and responding to questions, making a need to get a move on and commitment.

13. Advanced NFTs in Web-Based Business:
Description: Incorporation of non-fungible tokens (NFTs) for interesting and undeniable computerized resources.
Impact: Restricted release of computerized items and collectibles gives another aspect to online trade.

14. Social Verification and Client-Created Content:
Description: Dependence on client audits, evaluations, and client-produced content.
Impact: Positive audits and bona fide client encounters impact buying choices.

Keeping up to date with these patterns is critical for organizations to stay cutthroat and measure up to the steadily changing assumptions of shoppers in the unique online business and retail scene. Businesses can adapt to changing consumer preferences and behaviors by incorporating novel strategies based on these trends.

Chapter 2: Strategic Planning for the Holiday Season

Making key arrangements for the Christmas season is fundamental for organizations intending to boost amazing open doors, interface with buyers, and accomplish their occasional goals. A comprehensive guide to strategic holiday planning is provided here:

1. Put forth clear objectives and targets:
Purpose: Set definite, attainable, and measurable objectives for the holiday season.
Actions: Recognize deal targets, client-obtaining objectives, or other key execution markers (KPIs).
Adjust objectives to generally business targets.

2. Figure out your crowd:
Purpose: Realize your ideal interest group's inclinations, ways of behaving, and assumptions during special times of the year.
Actions: Break down past Christmas season information.

Lead overviews or accumulate criticism to figure out client assumptions.

3. Survey Past Execution:
Purpose: Gain from past special seasons to illuminate your system.
Actions: Perform an analysis of campaign performance, customer feedback, and sales data.
Find out what works and what can be done better.
4. Contender Examination:
Purpose: Comprehend what contenders are doing and recognize regions for separation.
Actions: Examine contenders' advertising techniques, advancements, and client commitment.
Recognize market gaps that your company can fill.

5. Multi-Channel Promotion System:
Purpose: Foster a durable methodology that traverses different channels for the most extreme reach.
Actions: Consolidate on the web and disconnected channels, including virtual entertainment, email advertising, and in-store advancements, and that's just the beginning.
Guarantee predictable information and marking across all channels.

6. Content Preparation:
Purpose: Engage your audience by creating content that is enticing and festive.
Actions: Plan occasion-themed content schedules for online entertainment, email crusades, and different channels.
Influence narrating to make close-to-home associations with your crowd.

7. Exceptional Advancements and Limits:

Purpose: Utilize appealing promotions and offers to entice customers.

Actions: Plan selective occasion limits, packaged arrangements, or restricted time advancements.

Consider faithfulness programs or early access for Rehash clients.

8. Upgrade Site and Client Experience:

Purpose: Make sure your online presence is prepared for more visitors.

Actions: Upgrade site speed and portable responsiveness.

Create a more user-friendly checkout process by streamlining it.

9. Stock preparation:

Purpose: Ensure that popular items are available and avoid stockouts.

Actions: Predict demand by analyzing data on previous sales.

Carry out compelling stock administration procedures.

10. Client care status:

Purpose: Prepare for an increase in support inquiries and customer inquiries.

Actions: Train client service groups for potential occasion-related questions.

Set up productive correspondence channels, including talk backing and web-based entertainment reactions.

11. Email Showcasing Efforts:

Purpose: Use email missions to connect with and convert clients.

Actions: Plan a progression of occasion-themed email crusades, including limited-time messages, bulletins, and customized proposals.

12. Measure and repeat:

Purpose: Ceaselessly screen execution and adjust systems in view of continuous information.

Actions: Carry out examination devices to follow key measurements.

Be ready to adjust based on how customers behave and how well the campaign is doing.

By decisively making arrangements for the Christmas season, organizations can situate themselves to actually contact their crowd, drive deals, and make paramount encounters that cultivate client dependability. This approach guarantees that the Christmas season turns into a time of development and accomplishment for the business.

Developing a Comprehensive Marketing Plan

A methodical approach to defining your marketing objectives, strategies, and tactics is necessary for the creation of a comprehensive marketing plan. Here is a bit-by-bit manual to assist you with making a powerful marketing plan:

1. Set clear targets: For your marketing efforts, establish specific, measurable, attainable, relevant, and time-bound (SMART) objectives.
Example: Increase online deals by 20% within the following quarter.

2. Figure out your ideal interest group: Recognize and profile your interest group, including socioeconomics, inclinations, and ways of behaving.
Direct statistical surveying to assemble bits of knowledge into purchaser requirements and assumptions.

3. SWOT Evaluation: Lead a SWOT examination (Qualities, Shortcomings, Potential Open Doors, Dangers) to evaluate

interior and exterior factors influencing your business. Recognize qualities to use, shortcomings to address, valuable chances to seek after, and dangers to alleviate.

4. Contender Examination: Dissect contenders to figure out market elements and distinguish regions for separation. Survey contenders' methodologies, assets, shortcomings, and market positioning.

5. Characterize Interesting Selling Suggestions (USP): Clearly state what distinguishes your product or service from those of your rivals. Make your distinctive value proposition stand out to the people you want to reach.

6. Showcasing Methodologies: To reach your goals, devise high-level strategies. Consider a blend of computerized and conventional marketing channels in view of your main interest group and industry.

7. Strategic Plans: Divide your strategies into campaigns and tactics that can be implemented. Incorporate subtleties like explicit channels (online entertainment, email, content promotion), financial plan distribution, and timetables.

8. Calendar of Contents: Make a substance schedule illustrating the subjects, configurations, and circulation plan for your substance showcasing endeavors. Adjust the content to your promotion objectives and address the necessities of your interest group.

9. Spending plan portion: Assign your showcasing spending plan

in view of the best channels and strategies. Consider the expense of promoting, content creation, innovation instruments, and different assets.

10. Four Ps of Marketing Mix: Survey and characterize your showcasing blend: item, value, spot, and advancement. Guarantee consistency in how your item or administration is introduced across all components.

11. Estimation Measurements: To assess your marketing efforts' success, establish key performance indicators (KPIs). Sales figures, conversion rates, website traffic, and social media engagement are all examples of metrics.
12. Execution Timetable: Foster a course of events illustrating how each showcasing strategy will be executed. Guarantee coordination among various groups and offices engaged with the execution.

13. Observing and Assessment: Always keep an eye on and evaluate how well your marketing campaigns are working. Use investigation apparatuses to assemble bits of knowledge and go with information-driven choices.

14. Transformation and Emphasis: Be ready to adjust your marketing plan in light of changing economic situations, buyer criticism, and mission execution. Ceaseless improvement is critical to long-term achievement.

15. Risk The board should recognize possible dangers and foster emergency courses of action. Expect difficulties and have procedures set up to relieve likely issues.

Keep in mind that a comprehensive marketing strategy is a living document that changes over time in response to changes in the market, how customers behave, and internal factors. Routinely return to and update your arrangement to remain spry and receptive to changes in the business climate.

Setting Clear Goals and Objectives

Laying out clear objectives and targets is a key stage in any essential arranging process, giving a guide to associations to accomplish their ideal results. A guide to clearly defining goals and objectives is provided below:

1. Figure out the distinction:
Goals: statements that define the organization's goals in general.
Example: Increment brand mindfulness.
Objectives: steps that are specific, measurable, and time-bound and help you reach your goals.
Example: Increase web-based entertainment commitments by 20% in the following quarter.

2. Line up with mission and vision: Check to see that the organization's goals and objectives are in line with its mission and vision.
This guarantees a strong and reason-driven way to deal with vital preparation.

3. Use SMART Standards: Make sure the objectives and goals are:
Specific: obviously characterized and nitty-gritty.
Measurable: quantifiable to follow progress.
Achievable: Practical and achievable.
Relevant: Lined up with generally speaking procedure.
Time-Bound: Set inside a particular time span.

4. Organize and Concentrate: To maintain focus and efficiency, set fewer goals. Focus on objectives in light of their importance to the association's prosperity.

5. Evaluate Where Conceivable: Whenever the situation allows, utilize quantitative measurements to gauge achievement. This makes it more straightforward to follow progress and assess results equitably.

6. Think about the present moment and long-haul objectives: Offset prompt goals with long-haul yearnings. Short-term objectives serve as bridges to more long-term, strategic goals.
7. Include key partners: Draw in important partners in the objective-setting process. This guarantees a common perspective and obligation to the association's targets.

8. Guarantee Consistency Across Offices: Objectives and goals ought to adjust across different divisions to advance cooperative energy and joint effort. A cross-useful arrangement guarantees that everybody is pursuing a common vision.

9. Audit and Overhaul Consistently: Check your goals on a regular basis and adjust them if necessary in response to changes in the external environment or organizational priorities. Flexibility is significant for remaining important and responsive.

10. Overflow Down the Association: Guarantee that objectives and targets are imparted and perceived at all levels of the

association.
This creates a sense of direction and course among colleagues.

11. Spur with Stretch Objectives: Include stretch goals that are challenging for teams and motivating without being too unrealistic. These objectives can drive development and pride.

12. Track and measure progress: Execute frameworks for following and estimating progress against set goals. Consistently break down information to evaluate whether objectives are being met.

13. Observe Accomplishments: Recognize and praise achievements and accomplishments en route. Acknowledgment makes everyone feel better and energizes them to proceed with devotion.

14. Gain from Mishaps: Consider setbacks as opportunities for growth and learning. Change methodologies in view of illustrations figured out how to upgrade future objective setting.

Organizations can set clear, attainable goals that guide their efforts and contribute to overall success by following these steps. Lucidity in an objective setting improves concentration, responsibility, and the probability of accomplishing desired results.

Allocating Budgets Effectively for Digital Campaigns

Designating spending plans for advanced crusades is vital for enhancing profit from ventures (return on capital invested) and accomplishing advertising objectives. This is an aid en route to distributing financial plans for computerized crusades:

1. Define the goals of the campaign: Obviously, frame the targets of your computerized crusade. Adjust spending plan designations to explicit objectives like lead age, brand mindfulness, or deals.

2. Figure out your crowd: Recognize and grasp your main interest group. Spend money on strategies and channels that most appeal to your audience's preferences and actions.

3. Use Information and Examination: Utilize data and analytics tools to comprehend how successful previous campaigns were. Designate a spending plan in view of the channels and strategies that have been shown to be best.

4. Execute the 70-20-10 Rule: Dispense 70% of the financial plan to demonstrated, generally safe systems.
Example: channels with a background marked by conveying a positive return for capital invested. Distribute 20% to methodologies with potential but less sureness.
Example: testing new promotion configurations or stages. Distribute 10% for testing or creative methodologies. Example: evaluating arising innovations or offbeat missions.

5. Channel Assignment: Circulate a financial plan across different computerized channels in light of your interest group and mission targets. Normal channels include:

- Virtual entertainment promotion

- Web crawler promotion (SEM)
- Email promotion
- Content-promoting
- Powerhouse organizations
- Show promotion

6. Take a Look at the Buyer's Journey: The budget should be strategically distributed across the stages of the buyer's journey (awareness, consideration, and decision). Change your spending in light of the stage that requires more accentuation for your particular mission.

7. Test and enhance: Put away a part of the financial plan for testing and streamlining. Persistently screen and investigate crusade execution, and change allotments in view of constant information.

8. Focus on High-Effect Strategies: Recognize high-influence strategies or channels that line up with your mission objectives. Dispense a relatively larger financial plan to these areas for the greatest effect.

9. Balance Paid and Natural Techniques: Think about a harmony among paid and natural methodologies. Dispense spending plan for paid crusades while additionally putting resources into natural endeavors like substance creation and Web optimization.

10. Represent Inventive and Promotion Creation: Apportion a spending plan for the production of convincing creatives and promotions.
Quality visuals and information altogether influence crusade adequacy.

11. Geographic and Segment Focusing on: In the event that material, apportion spending plan in view of geographic and segment focusing on.
Tailor missions to explicit areas or crowd portions for expanded significance.

12. Seasonal Changes: Think about occasional variances and change spending plan allotment likewise.
Assign more financial planning during the top seasons or when explicit occasions line up with your mission.

13. Screen Promotion Spend Effectiveness: Consistently screen the productivity of your promotion spend.
Use measurements like expense per click (CPC), cost per change, and return on promotion spend (ROAS) to assess viability.

14. Adaptability for Redistribution: Keep up with adaptability in your spending plan distribution.
Be prepared to redistribute reserves in light of the presentation of different diverts or surprising changes on the lookout.

15. Assess and Report: After the mission finishes up, consider the outcomes in contrast to the underlying financial plan distribution.
Create reports to examine the return on initial capital investment and accumulate bits of knowledge for future missions.

By decisively designating financial plans for computerized crusades, organizations can upgrade their showcasing endeavors, arrive at their target audience, and accomplish desired crusade results. Standard assessment and transformation in view of execution information are critical to boosting the effect of advanced showcasing speculations.

Chapter 3: Social Media Marketing Strategies

Online entertainment advertising methodologies include utilizing social stages to advance items, administrations, or brand messages. Engaging the intended audience, increasing brand awareness, and driving desired actions are the goals of these strategies. Here is an outline of key web-based entertainment advertising techniques:

1. Characterize Clear Goals: Lay out unambiguous and quantifiable objectives for your virtual entertainment-promoting endeavors.
Normal targets incorporate expanding brand mindfulness, driving site traffic, creating leads, or supporting deals.

2. Figure out Your Crowd: Distinguish and figure out your ideal interest group.

Make purchaser personas that fit content and inform explicit socioeconomics, interests, and ways of behaving.

3. Pick Applicable Stages: Select web-based entertainment stages that line up with your interest group and business objectives.
Well-known stages incorporate Facebook, Instagram, Twitter, LinkedIn, Pinterest, and TikTok.

4. Content Preparation and Creation: Foster a substance procedure that incorporates a blend of connecting with different kinds of content. Create content calendars with consistency and variety in mind.

5. Commitment and Local Area Building: Cultivate commitment by answering remarks, messages, and client-created content. Encourage user participation and conversations to build community around your brand.

6. Partnerships with Influencers: Team up with powerhouses who line up with your image and interest group. Powerhouses can intensify your message and provide valid support.

7. Paid Promotion: Make use of the options for paid advertising on social media platforms. Run designated promotions to contact explicit crowd sections in view of socioeconomics, interests, and ways of behaving.

8. Hashtag Systems: Encourage user-generated content and create branded hashtags. Exploration and influence of moving hashtags to grow reach and perceivability.

9. Reliable branding: Keep up with steady marking across all online entertainment channels. Utilize durable visuals, information, and tone to support brand character.

10. Examination and Observing: Screen an online entertainment examination to quantify the presentation of your missions. Keep tabs on important metrics like follower growth, reach, conversion rates, and engagement.

Web-based entertainment advertising techniques ought to be dynamic, advancing in view of stage changes, crowd ways of behaving, and industry patterns. The key is to fabricate major areas of strength for a presence, interface genuinely with your crowd, and accomplish your business goals through the essential utilization of web-based entertainment channels.

Leveraging Platforms for Increased Brand Visibility

Utilizing stages for expanded brand perceivability includes decisively using different internet-based channels to upgrade your image's presence and contact a more extensive crowd. This is an aid while heading to use various stages for expanded brand perceivability:

1. Platforms for social media: Make use of well-known social media platforms like TikTok, Facebook, Twitter, and LinkedIn. Make and offer drawings that line up with every stage's crowd and highlights.

2. Site design improvement (website optimization): Advance your site and content for web search tools to work on natural perceivability. Utilize applicable

catchphrases, enhance meta labels, and guarantee your site is dynamic.

3. Marketing via Content: Foster a substance system that incorporates blog entries, articles, recordings, and infographics. On platforms like LinkedIn, Medium, and your website, share content that is valuable and easy to share.

4. Email Showcasing: To regularly communicate with your audience, build and maintain an email subscriber list. Share updates, advancements, and important substance through designated email crusades.

5. Force to be reckoned with joint efforts: Cooperate with powerhouses in your industry or specialty to extend your image's scope. Powerhouses can acquaint your image with their supporters and give true support.

6. Podcasting: Begin a web recording or work together with existing digital broadcasts in your industry. Web recordings offer a special and individual method for interfacing with your crowd.

7. Online Surveys and Tributes: Encourage satisfied clients to post glowing reviews on sites like Yelp, Google My Business, or specific industry review sites. Reviews that are favorable increase visibility and credibility.

8. Organizations and joint efforts: Team up with different brands, associations, or powerhouses for joint missions. Organizations can acquaint their image with new crowds.

9. Online Gatherings and Networks: Partake in applicable web-based gatherings, conversation gatherings, or local area stages. Share your ability and draw in with likely clients.

10. Google My Business: Enhance your Google My Business profile to show up in nearby searches. Guarantee precise business data, transfer excellent pictures, and empower surveys.

11. Visual Stages (Pinterest, YouTube): Influence visual stages like Pinterest and YouTube. Make outwardly engaging substances, for example, infographics, instructional exercises, or item shows.

12. Visitor Writing for a Blog: Contribute visitor presents on legitimate websites or industry distributions. Visitor writing for a blog lays out power and acquaints your image with another crowd.

13. Events and webinars held online: To demonstrate your expertise and interact with your audience, host webinars or virtual events. Stages like Zoom or online class explicit stages can assist with working with these occasions.

14. Local area Commitment: Engage actively in online communities relevant to your sector or niche. Partake in conversations, answer questions, and offer significant experiences.

15. Use Paid Promoting: Put resources into paid publicizing on stages like Google Advertisements, Facebook Promotions, or Instagram Advertisements. To get the

most exposure, focus on particular interests and demographics.

16. Cross-Promotion: Cross-advance substances or missions across various stages. Repurpose blog content for social media, for instance, or share Instagram clips from a YouTube video.

17. Screen Examination: Routinely screen examination and execution measurements for every stage. Change your methodology in light of what stages and content resonate most with your crowd.

Utilizing different stages, all things considered, fortifies your image's perceivability and guarantees you arrive at your interest group across various internet-based channels. Adjust your methodology in light of the exceptional elements and crowd inclinations of every stage to expand your image's effect.

Crafting Engaging Content and Campaigns

Making drawings in Happy and Crusades includes making convincing, important, and shareable material to catch the attention of your ideal interest group. This is an aide while heading to make content and missions that resound with your crowd:

1. Figure out Your Crowd: Lead careful crowd exploration to figure out their inclinations, interests, and trouble spots. Tailor your substance to address the necessities and inclinations of your main interest group.

2. Characterize clear goals: Clearly frame the objectives and goals of your substance and missions. Whether it's rising image

mindfulness, driving site traffic, or producing leads, having clear targets directs your substance creation.

3. Make Convincing Titles and Snares: Create eye-catching titles and snares to allure your crowd. Use interest, humor, or feeling to make your crowd want to investigate further.

4. Recount a Story: Use narrating to make a story that reverberates with your crowd. Stories inspire feelings and make your substance more vital.

5. Visual Allure: Consolidate outwardly engaging components, like great pictures, infographics, and recordings. Visual substance stands out and improves the general client experience.

6. Intelligent Substance: Make intuitive substances like tests, surveys, or challenges to draw in your crowd. Intelligent components empower cooperation and make your substance more shareable.

7. Instructive Worth: Give significant and instructive substance that tends to your crowd's trouble spots or questions. Establish your brand as an industry authority.

8. Reliable branding: Make sure your branding is the same across all of your content. Utilize reliable varieties, text styles, and information to support brand personality.

9. Use Humor and Character: Infuse humor and character into your substance when appropriate. Acculturating your image makes it more appealing and important.

10. Dynamic Substance: Guarantee your substance is improved for cell phones. With a developing, versatile crowd, dynamic substance is fundamental for client commitment.

11. Content that is segmented and customized: Portion your crowd and make customized content in view of their inclinations. Personalization improves pertinence and increases commitment.

12. Make Evergreen Substance: Create content that is evergreen and relevant over time. Evergreen substances offer progressive benefits and can be reused across different channels.

13. Source of inspiration (CTA): Remember clear and convincing invitations to take action for your substance. Guide your crowd on the following stages, whether it's making a buy, buying in, or sharing the substance.

14. Engage in a Variety of Ways: Use various channels to disseminate your substance, including virtual entertainment, email, and sites; from there, the sky is the limit. Adjust your substance configuration to suit the stage and crowd conduct.

15. Input and Cycle: Empower criticism from your crowd and examine execution measurements. Utilize insights to iterate and enhance subsequent campaigns and content.

16. Client-Produced Content: Urge your crowd to make and share content connected with your image. The client created content from the local area and trust.

17. Test and Trial: A/B test various components of your substance, like titles, visuals, or CTA buttons. Trial and error distinguishes what resounds best with your crowd.

18. Social Verification: Integrate social verification, for example, client tributes or contextual investigations. Social confirmation fabricates belief and trust.

19. Remain Popular: Make your content relevant by keeping an eye on industry trends. Popular substances can stand out and show your image's importance.

20. Measure and Examine: Use investigation apparatuses to quantify the exhibition of your substance. Examine information to comprehend what functions admirably and refine your procedure likewise.

Making connections with content and missions is a continuous cycle that requires a profound comprehension of your audience and a pledge to convey esteem. You can strengthen your connections with your audience and achieve your marketing objectives by consistently producing content that is interactive, relevant, and of high quality.

Utilizing Social Commerce Features

Using social business highlights includes utilizing online entertainment stages to work with and improve the trading of items or administrations. Social business coordinates online business functionalities into web-based entertainment conditions, creating a consistent shopping experience for clients. The following are important aspects of using social commerce features:

1. Shoppable Posts: Empower shoppable posts via online entertainment stages like Instagram, Facebook, and Pinterest. Clients can find and buy items straightforwardly from posts, working on the purchasing system.

2. Descriptions and tags for products: Use item labels and point-by-point portrayals to provide fundamental data inside virtual entertainment posts. Without having to leave the platform, this enables users to make educated purchasing decisions.

3. In-Application Buys: Coordinate in-application buying abilities via online entertainment stages. Clients can finish exchanges without being diverted to an external site.

4. Shopping Inventories: Make and feature item inventories on stages like Facebook and Instagram. A variety of products are easily accessed and purchased by users.

5. Live Retail: Influence live shopping highlights for constant commitment. Organize live video sessions that feature product demonstrations and links to online shopping for viewers.

6. Social Suggestions: Urge clients to impart their number one items or buys to their informal communities. In social commerce, word-of-mouth recommendations play a significant role.

7. Client Surveys and Appraisals: Social media should directly incorporate ratings and reviews from customers. Positive input constructs trust and believability, affecting expected purchasers.

8. Increased Reality (AR) Attempt Ons: Execute AR highlights, permitting clients to take a stab at items essentially. This is particularly important for design, magnificence, and frill.

9. Restricted Time Offers and Glimmer Deals: Make use of the urgency of last-minute deals and flash sales to increase engagement and sales. Promoting deals that need to be done right away is easy on social media platforms.

10. Visit and Inform for Client Assistance: Use social media to directly integrate chat and messaging features for customer support. Brief reactions improve the general client experience.

11. Encourage users to share their experiences through user-generated content (UGC). Repurpose user-generated content for social commerce to demonstrate actual product usage.

12. Integration with platforms for e-commerce: Guarantee consistent reconciliation with internet business stages like Shopify or WooCommerce. This smooths out stock administration and request handling.

13. Cross-Advancements and Organizations: Work together with powerhouses or different brands for cross-advancements. Joint missions can extend their reach and draw in new clients.

14. Responsive Plan for Portable Clients: Advance social business highlights for portable clients. Numerous clients access web-based entertainment stages on their cell phones, so we guarantee a responsive and easy-to-understand plan.

15. Social Advertisements with Direct Buy Connections: In your social media ads, include links to make a direct purchase. Clients can go from seeing a promotion to making a purchase with insignificant snaps.

16. Mix of Social Installment Frameworks: Investigate the incorporation of social installment frameworks. A few stages offer in-application installment choices for a smoother checkout process.

17. Faithfulness Projects and Rewards: Carry out steadfastness projects or prizes for social business clients. Motivating forces can empower rehash buys and brand unwaveringness.

18. Information Investigation for Improvement: Influence information investigation to follow and break down client conduct on friendly business highlights. Use bits of knowledge

to upgrade item contributions and further develop the general shopping experience.

Social trade includes consistently advancing, and remaining refreshed with stage capacities and client inclinations is vital for effective execution. Businesses can make their audience's shopping experience more engaging and convenient by seamlessly integrating shopping functions into social media.

Chapter 4: Email Marketing Excellence

Email advertising greatness includes making and executing compelling email missions to connect with, sustain, and convert your crowd. Here are key standards and systems to accomplish greatness in email advertising:

1. Fabricate a Quality Email Rundown: Center around building a consent-based email list with endorsers who have enthusiastically picked in. Cleanse and segment your list frequently for personalized and targeted communication.

2. Segmentation and Personalization: Send emails to specific subscribers based on information like their name, preferences, or previous interactions. Send messages to specific segments of your audience to ensure relevance and engagement.

3. Convincing Headlines: Make eye-catching and important headlines to allure beneficiaries to open your messages. A convincing title expands the possibilities of your messages being perused.

4. Design that Responds: Guarantee your messages are portable and receptive to give a consistent encounter across gadgets. A dynamic plan further develops lucidity and client experience.

5. Clear CTA (call to action): Include a CTA that directs recipients to take the desired action and is compelling and clear. Make CTAs conspicuous and straightforward.

6. Connecting with Content: Create content that resonates with your audience and adds value. Utilize a blend of enlightening, engaging, and special substances to keep supporters locked in.

7. The A/B Test: Conduct A/B testing on various email components, including subject lines, content, and CTAs. Test and improve to find out what works best for your audience.

8. Timing and Recurrence: Consider the timing and recurrence of your email crusades. To determine when your audience is most responsive, test various days and times.

9. Mechanized Work Processes: Carry out computerized work processes for customized and ideal correspondences. Computerization can incorporate welcome messages, support arrangements, and deserted truck updates.

10. Email Examination: Consistently dissect email investigations to figure out crusade execution. For insights, keep an eye on metrics like open rates, click-through rates, and conversion rates.

11. List Support: Routinely spotless your email list by eliminating idle or withdrew contacts. Keep a solid and connected support base.

12. Consistence with Guidelines: Ensure that email marketing laws like CAN-SPAM and GDPR are followed. Provide simple ways to unsubscribe and obtain explicit consent.

13. Customized Greeting Pages: For a scamless user experience, link your personalized landing pages to your emails. Consistency between the email and point of arrival supports your message.

14. Responsive client assistance: email customer service that is responsive. Address requests and concerns instantly to build trust with your crowd.

15. Criticism and Overviews: Empower criticism and direct reviews to figure out supporters inclinations. Use bits of knowledge to refine your email technique.

16. Reconciliation with Different Channels: Incorporate your email advertising endeavors with different channels like web-based entertainment and content showcasing. A strong

multichannel approach reinforces your general showcasing system.

17. Persistent Learning and Transformation: Remain refreshed on industry drifts and arising emails promoting innovations. Adjust your technique in view of changing buyer conduct and innovation headways.

A combination of strategic planning, creativity, and data-driven optimization is required to achieve excellence in email marketing. By reliably conveying significant substance, customizing interchanges, and remaining receptive to supporter needs, you can identify areas of strength for assembling and driving significant outcomes through your email crusades.

Building Targeted and Personalized Email Campaigns

Building designated and customized email crusades includes fitting your messages to explicit portions of your audience to expand significance and commitment. This is an aid while heading to make viable designated and customized email crusades:

1. Fragment Your Crowd: Divide your email list into groups based on things like demographics, how people behave, or what they've bought in the past. You can send more targeted content to specific groups with segmentation.

2. Utilize Dynamic Substance: Include dynamic content in your emails that adapts to the characteristics of the recipient. Tailor pictures, text, or offers progressively to match the inclinations of each portion.

3. Customize Email Duplication: In the email copy, address recipients by their names. Add additional personalized information, such as a user's location, preferences, or previous purchases, by utilizing personalization tags.

4. Social Triggers: Set up mechanized messages set off by unambiguous client ways of behaving, for example, deserted trucks, site visits, or email clicks. Communication that is relevant and timely is ensured by behavioral triggers.

5. Buy History Suggestions: Give customized item suggestions in view of the beneficiary's previous buy history. Feature related or reciprocal items to energize extra buys.

6. Offers and Promotions Segmented: tailor advancements and offers in view of each section's inclinations. Various fragments might answer better to select limits, early access, or packaged bargains.

7. Content that is time-sensitive and localized: Tweak content in view of the beneficiary's area. Incorporate time-touchy data like neighborhood occasions, occasions, or restricted time offers.

8. Review and Input Solicitations: Send studies or input solicitations to grasp client inclinations and feelings. Utilize insights to further refine your personalization and targeting strategies.

9. Client Lifecycle Messages: Make designated messages for various phases of the client lifecycle. Welcome messages, sustain groupings, and dedication prizes can be customized for each stage.

10. Inclination Focuses: Permit endorsers to deal with their inclinations through inclination communities. Empower

supporters to pick the sort and frequency of messages they need to get.

11. Re-Commitment Missions: Distinguish latent supporters and send re-commitment crusades with customized content. Urge them to make a move or update their inclinations.

12. Design that Responds: Guarantee your messages are versatile and receptive to give a predictable encounter across gadgets. A versatile plan is pivotal for conveying customized content.

13. Customized Greeting Pages: Stretch out personalization to presentation pages connected to your messages. A consistent change from email to a customized presentation page supports your message.

14. Intelligent Substance: Incorporate intelligent components like tests, surveys, or reviews in your messages. Participation in interactive content yields useful information for further personalization.

15. Test and Enhance: A/B test various aspects of your customized emails. Based on what resonates most with each segment, analyze the results and adjust your strategy accordingly.

16. Mix with Client Information Stages (CDPs): Integrate your customer data platforms with your email marketing platform. Concentrated information empowers more thorough personalization across channels.

17. Security and Assent: Focus on protection and get unequivocal assent for personalization endeavors. Follow applicable information security guidelines to construct trust with your crowd.

18. Continual Development: Analyze performance metrics on a regular basis and collect feedback. Constantly refine your focus and personalization procedures in view of advancing client inclinations.

Building focused on and customized email crusades cultivates a more profound association with your audience by conveying content that reverberates with their singular requirements and inclinations. You can develop an email marketing strategy that is both more meaningful and more successful by making use of segmentation, dynamic content, and behavioral triggers.

Implementing Special Holiday Promotions

Carrying out exceptional occasion advancements includes making and executing designated promotional efforts during happy seasons to draw in clients, help deals, and upgrade brand perception. This is an aide en route to executing extraordinary occasion advancements, really:

1. Plan Ahead of Time: Start arranging your vacation advancements well ahead of time to guarantee a thoroughly examined technique. Think about significant occasions, seasons, and far-reaching developments pertinent to your interest group.

2. Figure out Your Crowd: Dissect your crowd's inclinations and ways of behaving during occasions. Tailor advancements to reverberate with the feelings and necessities of your particular crowd sections.

3. Make Restricted Time Offers: Produce a need to keep moving by presenting restricted time offers and advancements. This urges clients to make purchases during the occasion time frame.

4. Limits and Packages: Offer alluring limits or make packaged bargains. Consider packaging related items or giving restrictive limits to occasion-themed items.

5. Elite Advancements for Endorsers: Reward your email supporters with selective advancements. Energize recruits by advancing extraordinary occasion bargains accessible just to endorsers.

6. Gifts or free shipping with your purchase: During the holiday season, think about providing free shipping. Incorporate an unconditional present with buys over a specific add-up to boost bigger exchanges.

7. Influence Online Entertainment: Use online entertainment stages to advance your vacation advancements. Make drawing in satisfied, share bubbly visuals, and run designated promotions to contact a more extensive crowd.

8. Make Happy Landing Pages: configuration-devoted presentation pages with a bubbly topic. Make sure that the landing page and your promotional emails or ads flow smoothly.

9. Gift Guides and Suggestions: Curate gift guides or give item proposals for the Christmas season. Assist clients with tracking down appropriate gifts for their friends and family.

10. Occasion-Themed Email Missions: Plan merry and outwardly engaging email crusades. Use occasion-themed illustrations, varieties, and information to catch attention.

11. Conduct giveaways or contests: Draw in your crowd with occasion-themed challenges or giveaways. Urge social sharing to increment brand perceivability.

12. Streak Deals and Everyday Arrangements: Present glimmering deals or everyday arrangements, paving the way for explicit occasions. Feature various items every day to keep up with the fervor.

13. Team up with Powerhouses: Promoting your holiday promotions requires collaborating with influencers. Forces to be reckoned with can create valid substance and contact new crowds.

14. Email Advertising Groupings: Foster email showcasing groupings for various periods of the Christmas season. Present prompt riser advancements, mid-season specials, and last-minute arrangements.

15. Screen Contender Advancements: Watch out for your rivals' vacation advancements. Guarantee your contributions are cutthroat while keeping up with your one-of-a kind incentive.

16. Portable Streamlining: Enhance your advancements for cell phones. Numerous clients shop on portable during the Christmas season, so a versatile encounter is fundamental.

17. Client Dependability Projects: Reward faithful clients with selective advantages or limits. Support rehash business and improve client maintenance.

18. Post-Occasion Advancements: Expand advancements into the post-occasion time frame. Consider blowouts or extraordinary proposals to benefit from the continued shopping movement.

19. Track and Breakdown Results: Screen the exhibition of your vacation advancements using an examination. Dissect key measurements to comprehend what functioned admirably and regions for development.

20. Offer Thanks: Show appreciation to your clients by offering thanks for your advancements. Consider including festive thank-you notes with purchases or sending thank-you emails.

Carrying out exceptional occasion advancements requires a blend of inventiveness, key preparation, and ideal execution. You can create memorable and successful campaigns that drive holiday sales and foster positive customer relationships by tailoring your promotions to the holiday spirit and preferences of your audience.

Optimizing Email Sequences for Customer Retention

In order to keep current customers engaged, informed, and loyal, an email sequence that is optimized for customer retention must be designed and implemented. This is an aide en route to successfully improving email groupings for client maintenance:

1. Portion Your Client Base: Section your clients in light of their inclinations, buying history, or commitment level. Tailor email arrangements to address the interesting necessities of each portion.

2. Welcome and Onboarding Series: Create an extensive series of welcome and onboarding emails for new customers. Acquaint them with your image, guide them on item utilization, and feature key highlights.

3. Customized Proposals: Use client information to give customized item suggestions. Exhibit things in light of their past purchases or by perusing history.

4. Instructive Substance: Share instructive substance that increases the value of your clients. Offer tips, instructional

exercises, or selective experiences connected with your items or industry.

5. Selective Advancements and Unwaveringness Prizes: Offer restrictive advancements or steadfastness awards to show appreciation. Cause clients to feel extraordinary by giving them remarkable limits or early admittance to deals.

6. Commemoration and Achievement Messages: Recognize client commemorations or achievements with your image. Praise the term of their participation or the commemoration of their most memorable purchase.

7. Overview and Criticism Messages: Surveys can be used to get feedback and learn more about how satisfied customers are. Use bits of knowledge to work on your items or administrations and improve the client experience.

8. Renewal Updates: For items with a time span of usability or consumable merchandise, send recharging updates. Guarantee clients never show out of their number one thing to incite reorders.

9. Opportunities for Upsells and Cross-Sales: Distinguish strategically pitching and upselling potential open doors in light of client conduct. Suggest correlative items or updates that line up with their inclinations.

10. Occasional and Occasion Messages: Integrate occasional or occasion-themed messages into your arrangements. To captivate and engage customers, align your messaging with the festive mood.

11. Re-Commitment Missions: Create re-engagement campaigns for customers who are not active. Send designated messages with restrictive offers or impetuses to win them back.

12. Client special features: Offer selective items, early access, or content to your devoted clients. Make them feel like they are a part of a small group.

13. Social Verification and Tributes: Share client tributes or examples of overcoming adversity in your groupings. Feature positive encounters to build trust and fulfillment.

14. Dynamic Substance: Execute dynamic substance that adjusts in view of client conduct. Show pertinent substance, like recently seen items or customized suggestions.

15. Shock and Pleasure Messages: To show your appreciation, send emails of surprise and delight. Offer startling prizes, limits, or customized messages to enchant clients.

16. Portable Streamlining: Guarantee your email arrangements are streamlined for cell phones. Numerous clients draw in with messages that are versatile, so a responsive plan is fundamental.

17. Reliable branding: Keep up with predictable marking across all messages. Utilize natural tones, textual styles, and symbolism to support your image's character.

18. The A/B Test: Lead A/B testing on different components of your email successions. To improve performance, test subject lines, content, and calls to action.

19. Integration of Customer Support: Give simple access to client assistance through your email arrangements. Incorporate connections or contact data for fast help.

20. Analyze and monitor metrics: Screen key measurements like open rates, navigate rates, and change rates. Investigate information to comprehend the viability of your email groupings and make information-driven enhancements.

You can strengthen your customer relationships, increase brand loyalty, and encourage repeat business by creating targeted and personalized email sequences. Routinely dissect and refine your email groupings in view of client criticism and execution measurements for ceaseless improvement.

Chapter 5: Search Engine Optimization (SEO) for the Holidays

Improving your site for web crawlers during special times of year is vital to drawing in occasional customers and increasing perceivability. A guide on how to use search engine optimization (SEO) during the holidays is provided below:

1. Watchword Exploration: Distinguish occasion-specific catchphrases connected with your items or administrations. Incorporate terms like "occasion bargains," "gift thoughts," or "merry limits" in your watchword technique.

2. Update Meta Labels: Improve meta titles and depictions with occasion-centered catchphrases. Make convincing and bubbly meta labels that support clicks.

3. Create content about the holidays: Foster occasion-themed blog entries, articles, and presentation pages. Address normal occasion-related questions and give important substance.

4. Improve Item Pages: Update item portrayals with occasion watchwords. Feature any extraordinary offers, limits, or packages conspicuously.

5. Portable Streamlining: Guarantee your site is versatile for clients on different gadgets. Google focuses on versatile destinations in its search rankings.

6. Further develop page burden speed: improve the user experience by speeding up your website. Quicker stacking pages will generally rank higher in query items.

7. Neighborhood Web Optimization: Upgrade for a neighborhood look, assuming that you have actual stores. Incorporate area-specific watchwords and update your Google My Professional reference.

8. Make a Gift Guide: Foster an occasion gift guide on your site. Streamline it for web search tools and incorporate connections to significant item pages.

9. Influence Online Entertainment: Advance-occasion content via virtual entertainment stages. Social signs can, in a roundabout way, influence web optimization.

10. Client-Produced Content: Urge clients to make and share occasion-related content. Client-produced content can upgrade your internet-based presence.

11. Carry out Blueprint Markup: Use pattern markup to give web crawlers extra information about your substance. This can upgrade rich bits in query items.

12. Update Google My Business: Keep your Google My Business profile refreshed with occasional hours and advancements. Nearby organizations can profit from further developed perceivability in neighborhood list items.

13. Backlink Building: Assemble pertinent and top-notch backlinks to your vacation content. Visitor posting, powerhouse joint efforts, and effort can contribute to backlink development.

14. Screen and Break Down Execution: Use instruments like Google Investigation to screen the exhibition of your vacation pages. Keep tabs on key metrics like traffic and conversion rates.

15. Enhance Images: Pack and enhance pictures on your site. This further develops page load times, adding to a positive client experience.

16. Make a Commencement: Add an occasion commencement on your site. Make a need to get moving, empowering clients to investigate and make purchases.

17. Organized Information Markup: Execute organized information markup for occasion-related occasions, advancements, or deals. Specific details may appear more prominently in search results as a result of this.

18. Screen Contender Methodologies: Keep an eye on the holiday SEO strategies of your rivals. Recognize regions where you can separate and move along.

19. Update URLs: On the off chance that they are relevant, update your URLs to reflect occasion-related catchphrases. Keep URLs compact and graphic.

20. Prepare for SEO after the holidays: Make plans for promotions and content after the holiday. Guarantee a

smooth change and progress in website design enhancement endeavors after the Christmas season.

To attract festive customers, optimizing your website for the holidays necessitates a well-thought-out strategy. You can increase the visibility of your website in search engine results and bring holiday-related traffic to your business by incorporating holiday keywords, creating seasonal content, and making sure users have a good experience.

Conducting Seasonal Keyword research

Directing occasional watchword research is the most common way of distinguishing and focusing on unambiguous catchphrases that are pertinent to a specific season. This training is essential for organizations planning to improve their internet-based content, promotion, and generally, computerized presence to line up with occasional patterns. This is an aide while heading to lead occasional catchphrase research:

1. Figure out Occasional Patterns: Recognize the pinnacle seasons and occasions applicable to your industry. Comprehend the particular terms and expressions related to these seasons.

2. Conceptualize Occasional Watchwords: Conceptualize a rundown of potential occasional catchphrases connected with your items or administrations. Consider both expansive and explicit terms that clients could use during the season.

3. Use Watchword Exploration Instruments: Use watchword research devices like Google Catchphrase Organizer, SEMrush, or Ahrefs. Enter your underlying rundown of occasional catchphrases to find extra-related terms and survey their inquiry volumes.

4. Investigate long-tail catchphrases: Search for long-tail watchwords that catch explicit inquiries connected with the season. Long-tail keywords typically have lower levels of competition and may be able to bring in more specific traffic.

5. Dissect Contender Catchphrases: Examine the catchphrases on which your rivals are focusing for the season. Recognize holes or chances to separate your methodology.

6. Think about nearby watchwords: For local search optimization, include location-specific keywords if applicable. Restricting your watchwords can be particularly significant for occasions or advancements attached to explicit areas.

7. Include Specific Holiday Terms: Incorporate occasion-specific terms related to the season. For example, "Christmas presents," "New Year's limits," or "summer getaway arrangements."

8. Represent Patterns and Subjects: Take into account the season's emerging trends and themes. Include keywords that represent topics or interests that were popular at the time.

9. Consider User Intent: Recognize the purpose of the phrases and keywords. Upgrade for instructive, navigational, or conditional inquiries in light of the client goal.

10. Make Occasional Presentation Pages: Create separate landing pages for your seasonal campaigns in your

plans. Enhance these pages with the chosen occasional watchwords.

11. Assess Authentic Information: Dissect verifiable information if accessible. Distinguish catchphrases that performed well during past seasons and consider advancing them once more.

12. Screen Search Patterns: Remain refreshed on ebb and flow search patterns connected with the season. Use instruments like Google Patterns to distinguish rising questions.

13. Use Occasional Modifiers: Incorporate modifiers that convey the occasional energy in your catchphrases. "Summer outside exercises," "bubbly occasion recipes," and so forth.

14. Bunch catchphrases Decisively: Arrange your watchwords into key gatherings or subjects. This smooths out your substance creation and enhancement endeavors.

15. Enhance for Voice Search: Consider how clients could state occasional questions in voice search. Improve your regular language and conversational catchphrases.

16. Test and refine: Monitor performance by putting your chosen seasonal keywords into practice. Use examinations to assess the adequacy of your catchphrase decisions and make changes on a case-by-case basis.

17. Think about Multi-Language Catchphrases: If relevant, remember watchwords for numerous dialects for

assorted crowds. Represent social and semantic varieties connected with the season.

18. Balance High and Low Contest Catchphrases: Figure out some kind of harmony between high-rivalry and low-contest watchwords. You can target both popular terms and niche opportunities with a mix.

19. Optimize Meta Descriptions and Tags: Integrate occasional catchphrases into meta labels and portrayals. This upgrades the perceivability of your substance in web search tool results.

20. Prepare for Content Creation: Make a schedule in advance for the creation of content. This guarantees you have upgraded content all set before the pinnacle of time.

By conducting exhaustive, occasional catchphrase research, you can adjust your advanced system to the interests and search conduct of your ideal interest group during explicit seasons. Your chances of making use of seasonal trends and events and attracting relevant traffic are improved by this optimization.

Optimizing Website Content for Festive Keywords

The process of strategically incorporating holiday-specific terms into your web pages in order to improve visibility, attract targeted traffic, and align with seasonal trends is known as optimizing website content for festive keywords. This is an aide while heading to streamline site content for merry catchphrases:

1. Recognize important Merry Watchwords: Lead a catchphrase examination to distinguish bubbly

watchwords applicable to your industry and items. Consider both general and explicit terms related to the Christmas season.

2. Update Meta Labels: Advance meta titles and portrayals with merry watchwords. Create convincing meta-labels that support clicks while integrating occasion terms.

3. Use Christmas-themed keywords in headings: Integrate happy catchphrases into your heading labels (H1, H2, and so on.). Make headings that are both happy and educational.

4. Streamline Item Portrayals: Update item portrayals with merry language and catchphrases. Feature any occasion-related highlights, advantages, or advancements.

5. Make Happy Points of Arrival: Create custom landing pages for festive events or promotions. Streamline these pages with merry catchphrases and give significant substance connected with the season.

6. Create Occasional Blog Content: Create articles or blog posts with holiday-themed themes. Address normal forms of feedback connected with the Christmas season.

7. Use Alt Text for Happy Pictures: Your website's alt text should include festive keywords. This improves availability and gives extra settings to web crawlers.

8. Feature Occasional Offers: Highlight any seasonal discounts, promotions, or offers prominently. Utilize bubbly catchphrases to underline the restricted time nature of these arrangements.

9. Consolidate client-created content: Customers should be encouraged to share festive content about your products. Highlight client-produced pictures or tributes on your site with suitable watchwords.

10. Streamline URLs: If appropriate, update your URLs to incorporate bubbly catchphrases. Keep URLs succinct, elucidating, and lined up with occasion-themed content.

11. Influence social verification: Incorporate happy tributes or surveys from fulfilled clients. Social confirmation adds believability and reverberates with expected purchasers.

12. Make Gift Guides: Create festive gift guides that are in line with your offerings. Enhance these aides for web crawlers with significant watchwords.

13. Upgrade for Nearby Pursuit: Assuming your business has actual areas, incorporate area-specific, bubbly catchphrases. Streamline for nearby pursuits to draw in occasion customers in your space.

14. Carry out Blueprint Markup: Use composition markup to give extra data about happy occasions, advancements, or items. Improve rich bits in list items to make them stand out.

15. Favor seasonal evaluations: Urge clients to leave audits explicitly referencing their vacation encounters. Positive, bubbly surveys can impact possible clients.

16. Make intuitive substance: Create happy tests, surveys, or intuitive substance. Draw in guests while consolidating bubbly watchwords normally.

17. Improve for Voice Search: Consider how clients could express happy questions in voice search. Improve content for conversational and regular language.

18. Unmistakably Show Bubbly Suggestions to Take Action (CTAs): Incorporate bubbly CTAs that guide guests to make explicit moves. Make it simple for clients to explore and draw in with your vacation-themed content.

19. Screen Contender Methodologies: Remain informed about how contenders are enhancing their catchphrases. Distinguish regions where you can separate or work on your methodology.

20. Consistently Update Content: Keep your substance new and important all through the Christmas season. Standard updates signify to web indexes that your webpage is effectively providing important data.

By decisively integrating merry catchphrases into your site content, you can improve its perceivability during special seasons and draw in guests explicitly looking for occasional items or data. Your digital presence will look more festive as a result of this optimization, which will also increase your chances of getting targeted traffic.

Building Backlinks and Citations

The improvement of your website's authority, search engine rankings, and online visibility all depend on the creation of backlinks and citations. This is an aide en route to really constructing backlinks and references:

Building Backlinks:

1. Make Excellent Substance: Foster important, educational, and shareable substance on your site. Great substance normally draws in backlinks.

2. Visitor Posting: Write guest posts for well-known websites in your field. In the author's bio or content, include a link to your website.

3. Connect for third-party referencing: Distinguish sites that could profit from connecting to your substance. Contact them with customized messages, displaying the worth of your substance.

4. Use broken Third-party referencing: Track down broken joins on different sites inside your specialty. Offer your substance as a substitution and solicit a connection.

5. Partake in Industry Discussions: Participate in gatherings and conversation sheets applicable to your industry. Incorporate your site into your discussion mark or, when suitable,.

6. Team up with Powerhouses: Join forces with powerhouses or industry specialists. Forces to be reckoned with can be connected to your substance, giving openness to their supporters.

7. Make Infographics: Configuration outwardly engaging infographics connected with your industry. Urge others to share and connect to your infographics.

8. Make use of social media: Use social media to share your content. Social signs can, by implication, add to web search tool rankings.

9. Assemble Associations with Bloggers: Meet bloggers who write about your subject. Propose to contribute content or team up on projects that normally incorporate backlinks.

10. Submit to catalogs: Present your site to significant professional resources. Guarantee that the catalogs are respectable and industry-explicit.

Building Citationeferences:

1. Guarantee Your Google My Professional Resource: Guarantee and enhance your Google My Business (GMB) posting. Guarantee exact and reliable business data.

2. Submit to Neighborhood Catalogs: List your business on neighborhood registries like Cry, Yellow Pages, and TripAdvisor. It is essential to have NAP information that is consistent.

3. Enhance Online Profiles: Make your business profiles on Facebook and LinkedIn look their best. Incorporate predictable business subtleties across all profiles.

4. Partake in Nearby Occasions: Participate in or sponsor local events. Being related to nearby occasions can prompt notices and references.

5. Work together with nearby complications: Collaborate with other local organizations and businesses. Notice each other on your sites, giving shared references.

6. Get Surveys and Tributes: Urge fulfilled clients to leave audits. Positive web-based audits can add to your business's validity.

7. Nearby News Inclusion: Look for inclusion in neighborhood media sources or local area distributions. Citations of businesses mentioned in online news articles are frequently included.

8. Make Area Explicit Substance: Foster substance well defined for your neighborhood. This can draw in neighborhood references and further develop relevance in nearby quests.

9. Partake in Neighborhood Sponsorships: Support nearby game groups, occasions, or local area drives. Sponsorship frequently prompts business notices and references.

10. Keep up with the information. Exactness: Routinely check and update your business data on the web. Mistaken information can prompt conflicting references.

Tips for Both Backlinks and References:

• Focus on higher standards without compromise: center around getting top-notch backlinks and references from legitimate sources.

• Broaden Anchor Text: To avoid over-optimization, acquire backlinks using a variety of anchor text.

• Remain Moral: Avoid spammy link-building techniques that go against the rules set by search engines.

• Screen and Dissect: Use apparatuses like Google Investigation to screen the effect of your backlinks and references. Change your procedure in view of execution information.

Building backlinks and references is a continuous cycle that requires constancy and an emphasis on offering some benefit to your audience. A different and regular connection profile adds to a more grounded internet-based presence and further develops web search tool rankings.

Chapter 6: Mobile Marketing Best Practices

Portable advertising is significant for coming to and connecting with crowds on cell phones and other cell phones. For successful mobile marketing, follow these best practices:

1. Design for Mobile Devices: Guarantee your site and messages are upgraded for cell phones. Make use of responsive design to create an experience that is consistent across screen sizes.

2. Quick Loading Time: Upgrade your portable site for speedy stacking times. Portable clients anticipate quick and effective encounters.

3. CTAs (clear calls to action): Utilize brief and convincing CTAs that are effectively tappable. Obviously, convey the ideal move you maintain that clients should make.

4. Work on Structures: Limit structure fields to diminish erosion. Dropdowns and checkboxes, which are mobile-friendly input options, may be considered.

5. Individualized messages: Make use of user data to tailor messages. Tailor content in view of client inclinations, area, and conduct.

6. Enhanced Emails: Configuration messages for versatile review. Utilize a single segment format, huge text dimensions, and contact-well-disposed buttons.

7. Area-Based Focusing on: Use area information for designated advancements. Send important offers or data in light of clients' geographic areas.

8. Intelligent Substance: Integrate intuitive components like tests, surveys, or swipeable pictures. Draw in clients with intuitive substance that suits versatile communications.

9. Versatile Publicizing Arrangements: Pick versatile promotion designs, like local advertisements or in-application promotions. Improve promotion creatives for more modest screens.

10. SMS Promoting: Carry out SMS advertising capably. Acquire assent prior to sending messages, and offer some benefit in your messages.

11. Portable Application Streamlining: Improve the performance and usability of your mobile application. Update the app frequently to address user feedback and enhance features.

12. Web-based Entertainment Enhancement: Improve virtual entertainment content for portable utilization. Utilize dynamic arrangements, for example, vertical recordings, on stages like Instagram and TikTok.

13. Consistency across channels: Ensure that the brand experience is the same across all channels. Keep a durable message and plan whether clients cooperate on portable, work area, or different stages.

14. Voice Inquiry Streamlining: Adjust content for voice search questions. Advance for normal language and long-tail watchwords.

15. Versatile Installment Choices: Work with portable installments for a smoother checkout process. Choose payment methods that are safe and simple to use.

16. Pop-up messages: Use message pop-ups wisely. Give significant updates, offers, or data to clients who have opted in.

17. Increased Reality (AR): Investigate AR encounters for versatile clients. AR can upgrade commitment and provide extraordinary communications.

18. Portable Investigation: Use versatile investigation apparatuses to follow client conduct. Learn how users interact with your mobile content and adjust your strategy accordingly.

19. Test Across Gadgets: Test your missions on different cell phones and working frameworks. Guarantee a reliable and positive experience across various stages.

20. Consistency with Guidelines: Respect regulations regarding data security and privacy. Get appropriate assent for gathering and utilizing client information.

By carrying out these prescribed procedures, you can think of a versatile promotion system that resounds with clients, conveys a positive encounter, and drives significant commitment. Monitor performance metrics on a regular basis, and adjust your strategy to keep up with mobile trends and user preferences.

Optimizing Website and Campaigns for Mobile Users

Streamlining your site and lobbies for versatile clients is significant for conveying a consistent and easy-to-understand insight. Here is a far-reaching guide on the best way to successfully improve for versatility:

1. Design that Responds: Make sure your website works on all screen sizes by using responsive design. Test your site's responsiveness across various gadgets.

2. Rapidly Loading: Advance pictures, limit HTTP demands, and influence program storing. Speed up stacking times to improve the client experience on versatile.

3. Dynamic Substance: Focus on succinct and effectively searchable substance for versatile clients. Separate the substance into short sections and use headings for clarity.

4. Instinctive Route: Improve route menus for simple access on more modest screens. Carry out natural symbols and clear suggestions to take action for a consistent route.

5. Streamlined Structures: Forms should be simplified and the number of fields reduced. Utilize dynamic information strategies like checkboxes and dropdowns.

6. Portable Inquiry Enhancement: Upgrade your site for portable inquiries. Center around neighborhood Web optimization and guarantee that your site shows up in portable query items.

7. Contact Well-Disposed Buttons: Plan huge and tappable buttons to work with contact communications. Make sure that users can tap buttons and links without making an error.

8. Versatile Pictures and Recordings: Pack pictures and utilize the proper document designs for versatility. Utilize responsive video players and guarantee recordings are upgraded for portable review.

9. Looking Over Plan: Create pages that encourage scrolling vertically. Stay away from unnecessary information, even when looking for a more easy-to-use insight.

10. Versatile Typography: Utilize versatile typography that changes with various screen sizes. Guarantee text stays lucid and readable on more modest screens.

11. Execute Sped Up Versatile Pages (AMP): Consider executing AMP to make quicker stacking versatile pages. AMP is especially helpful for websites that focus on content.

12. Cross-Program Similarity: Test your site across different portable programs. Ensure that performance and appearance are consistent across browsers.

13. Portable Application Streamlining: On the off chance that you have a versatile application, upgrade its exhibition and UI. Guarantee smooth progress between your site and the versatile application.

14. Area-Based Improvement: Use geolocation highlights for customized encounters. Offer area-based content or advancements to upgrade significance.

15. Moderate Web Application (PWA): Think about making a PWA for better mobile functionality. PWAs give users an app-like experience without requiring them to install anything.

16. Client Testing: Direct ease-of-use testing with genuine, versatile clients. Assemble criticism on the versatile experience and make enhancements in like manner.

17. Online Entertainment Reconciliation: Create content that is optimized for social media sharing. Utilize versatile arrangements for pictures and recordings on friendly channels.

18. Portable Investigation: Use versatile investigation apparatuses to follow client conduct. Acquire bits of knowledge about how clients collaborate with your versatile substance and missions.

19. Campaigns on mobile that are customized: Adapt your mobile campaigns to the preferences and actions of your audience. User engagement and conversion rates increase with personalization.

20. Consistence with Portable Guidelines: Keep up with the latest mobile guidelines and standards. Make sure that the rules and best practices for the mobile industry are followed.

By deliberately streamlining your site and lobbies for portable clients, you can create a positive and client-driven, versatile experience. Routinely screen examination, look for client input, and adjust your way to deal with stay lined up with advancing versatile patterns and advancements.

Leveraging SMS Marketing for Promotions

Utilizing SMS showcasing for advancements can be a strong approach to drawing in your crowd straightforwardly. This is an aide while heading to involve SMS for advancements successfully:

1. Fabricate a consent-based rundown: Before sending promotional SMS, explicitly ask users for their permission. Make it abundantly clear to them what they will gain from signing up.

2. Fragment Your Crowd: Fragment your SMS list in view of socioeconomics, inclinations, or past collaborations. Send designated advancements to explicit fragments for expanded significance.

3. Create Convincing Messages: Keep SMS messages brief and convincing. Obviously, impart the advancement, its advantages, and any fundamental subtleties.

4. Timing Matters: Think about the planning of your SMS advancements. Abstain from sending messages during late hours and pick ideal days for your crowd.

5. Personalization: Utilize the recipient's name to personalize SMS messages. Make promotions based on previous interactions or purchases.

6. Incorporate a Reasonable Source of Inspiration (CTA): Obviously express the move you believe that beneficiaries should make. Utilize noteworthy language and give a clear CTA.

7. Offer some benefit: Guarantee your advancements offer certified worth to beneficiaries. Select limits, early access, or restricted-time offers can constrain.

8. Restricted Time Offers: Make a need to keep moving with restricted time advancements. To take advantage of the offer, encourage immediate action.

9. Improve for Versatile: Plan SMS advancements in view of cell phones. Make sure that it is easy to read and that using your phone is easy.

10. Link to landing pages optimized for mobile: In the event that is pertinent, incorporate connections to dynamic points of arrival. Make sure that the SMS-to-website transition is easy.

11. Two-Way Correspondence: Allow your SMS recipients to respond or engage. Enable two-way communication for inquiries and feedback from customers.

12. Measure and examine: Track the exhibition of your SMS advancements. Screen open rates, navigate rates, and change measurements.

13. Consistence with Guidelines: Ensure that SMS marketing regulations are followed. Incorporate quit choices and regard client inclinations.

14. Utilize Short Codes: For easier recall, think about using short codes. Short codes work on the cycle for clients to draw in with your advancements.

15. Reconciliation with Different Channels: SMS promotions should be part of your overall marketing plan. For a cohesive approach, collaborate with email, social media, and other channels.

16. Client Dependability Projects: Integrate SMS advancements into client steadfastness programs. Rehash clients with selective offers.

17. Geo-Designated Advancements: Use area-based focusing for SMS advancements. Send offers or cautions in view of the beneficiary's geographic area.

18. Robotize SMS Missions: Execute robotization for planned SMS crusades. Make use of automation tools to keep things consistent and speed up the process.

19. The A/B Test: Try different things with A/B testing for various components of your SMS advancements. Test varieties of messages, timing, and offers to upgrade results.

20. Post-Advancement Follow-Up: Circle back to beneficiaries after the advancement lapses. Assemble criticism, offer thanks, or offer forthcoming advancements.

By following these prescribed procedures, you can use SMS showcasing as an important device for advancing your items or administrations, encouraging client commitment, and driving transformations. Keep in mind to adjust your strategy in response to user feedback and changing industry trends.

Implementing Mobile-Friendly Ad Campaigns

Ad campaigns that are compatible with mobile devices are essential if you want to reach and engage users on a variety of mobile devices. The following is a guide to creating mobile-friendly advertising campaigns:

1. Grasp Your Versatile Crowd: Find out how your target audience uses mobile devices by analyzing them. Distinguish the gadgets, working frameworks, and screen measures your crowd generally utilizes.

2. Responsive Promotion Plan: Make promotions with a responsive plan that adjusts to various screen sizes. Guarantee clarity and visual allure on more modest screens.

3. Upgrade Promotion Duplicate Length: Keep promotion duplication succinct and effective. Catch consideration rapidly, as portable clients frequently have restricted time and capacities to focus.

4. Versatile Explicit Promotion Augmentations: Make use of mobile-specific ad extensions. Incorporate highlights like snap-to-call, application augmentations, or area expansions for upgraded portable collaborations.

5. Clear CTA (call to action): Highlight a reasonable and convincing CTA in your promotion. Urge clients to make explicit moves pertinent to their portable experience.

6. Portable Advanced Points of Arrival: Guarantee that greeting pages connected to advertisements are versatile and streamlined. Keep a reliable visual subject and client experience from promotion to presentation page.

7. Versatile Promotion Arrangements: Pick promotion designs that are helpful for portable surveys. Mobile ads can be effective in carousel, video, and interactive formats.

8. Visual Allure: Utilize outwardly engaging pictures or recordings in your versatile advertisements. Guarantee that visuals are drawing in and pass on your message really.

9. Streamline Stacking Pace: Upgrade promotion components for quick stacking times. Quicker stacking speeds add to a positive client experience.

10. Particularly Target Mobile Devices: Section your promotion missions to expressly target cell phones. Change offering methodologies and spending plans in view of the exhibition on versatility.

11. Use Portable Promotion Organizations: Investigate promoting on portable explicit organizations. Stages like Facebook, Instagram, and Google Promotions offer versatile publicizing choices.

12. Influence in-application promotion: If pertinent to your crowd, consider in-application promotion. Advertise within mobile applications to reach users in the settings they prefer.

13. Localize the ad content: Confine promotion content in light of the client's area. Tailor advancements or messages to suit nearby inclinations or occasions.

14. Iterate and Test: Execute A/B testing for various promotion creatives and duplicate. Use execution information to refine and streamline your portable promotion crusades.

15. Cross-Gadget Consistency: Keep a steady brand insight across gadgets. Guarantee that versatile promotion crusades line up with your general marking methodology.

16. Geo-Targeting: Geo-targeting lets you reach users in specific areas. Ad content can be tailored to the user's location.

17. Intelligent Components: Consolidate intelligent components in your versatile advertisements. Urge clients to swipe, tap, or draw in with your promotion content.

18. Portable Inquiry Enhancement: Upgrade promotion content for versatile pursuits. Comprehend how clients state questions on cell phones, and designer promotion duplicates likewise.

19. Virtual Entertainment Promoting: Influence web-based entertainment stages for versatile promotion. Use the focus on choices accessible on stages like Instagram, Twitter, and LinkedIn.

20. Screen and examine measurements: Track key measurements like navigation rates, changes, and commitment. Investigate execution information to make information-driven adjustments to your versatile promotion crusades.

By carrying out these systems, you can make dynamic promotion crusades that actually reach and draw in your interest group on their favorite gadgets. Consistently screen execution measurements and adjust your way to deal with them to stay aligned with developing versatile patterns.

Chapter 7: Creative and Innovative Campaigns

Making inventive and creative missions can separate your image and catch the attention of the crowd. Here are methodologies to inject imagination into your promotional efforts:

1. Narrating Efforts: Make convincing stories that resonate with your crowd. To make an emotional connection, use storytelling across various media.

2. Client-Created Content (UGC) Missions: Urge clients to make content connected with your image. Display user-generated content to foster community and authenticity.

3. Intelligent Encounters: Create campaigns that are interactive, such as contests, polls, or quizzes. Draw in your crowd and make them dynamic members of the mission.

4. Expanded Reality (AR) Missions: Explore augmented reality to create immersive experiences. Add augmented reality (AR) elements to your campaigns for a novel and distinctive touch.

5. Guerrilla Showcasing: Use marketing strategies that are out of the ordinary and unanticipated. Make paramount encounters that create buzz and online entertainment considerations.

6. Cause Promoting Efforts: Adjust your image to a social or ecological reason. Understand your obligation to have a constructive outcome.

7. Restricted Time Offers and Glimmer Deals: With promotions that expire soon, elicit a sense of urgency. Energize prompt activity from your crowd.

8. Forces to be reckoned with joint efforts: Work with influencers who share your brand's values. Work together on creative campaigns and content that makes use of their reach.

9. Customized Encounters: Tailor crusades in light of client inclinations and conduct. Influence information to give customized and significant substance.

10. Experiential Showcasing: Have live occasions or vivid encounters. Associate with your crowd in an unmistakable and significant manner.

11. Gamification Missions: Consolidate game-like components in your missions. To increase engagement, create challenges, rewards, or interactive elements.

12. Unpacking Efforts: Benefit from the fervor of unpacking encounters. Make outwardly engaging bundling and urge clients to share their unpacking minutes.

13. Producing Content Together: Create content together with your audience. Publicly support thoughts, stories, or pictures for an aggregate mission.

14. Trend jacking: Take part in or adjust to the latest things. To stay relevant, produce content that is in line with current topics.

15. 360-Degree Video Missions: Utilize 360-degree recordings for vivid narrating. Give an intelligent and all-encompassing perspective to your crowd.

16. Invert Advertising: Flip around customary advertising draws near. Challenge shows and make crusades that stand apart through inversion.

17. Secret Campaigns: Assemble tension with secret missions. Bother your crowd with interesting clues prior to uncovering the full mission.

18. Embrace Wistfulness: Tap into nostalgic components that resound with your crowd. Make crusades that bring out good recollections or sentiments.

19. Customization and Personalization: Allow customers to personalize services or products. Customized crusades improve commitment and association.

20. Virtual and Expanded Reality Channels: Foster channels for well-known online entertainment stages. Empower clients to connect with your image through AR channels.

Make sure to persistently investigate the progress of your missions, assemble input, and adjust your techniques in light of crowd reaction and developing patterns. Imagination frequently implies facing challenges, so go ahead and try different things with new and striking thoughts.

Showcasing Successful Campaigns from Previous Seasons

While I can't give constant or explicit missions, I can feature different kinds of effective missions from different businesses in past seasons:

1. The Share a Coke campaign from Coca-Cola: Consumer engagement was enhanced by personalized labels that included individual names. Urged clients to share their customized Coke bottles via online entertainment.

2. Nike's Fantasy Insane Mission: Including Colin Kaepernick, it resolved social issues and roused a strong message. It ignited discussions and got positive reactions for its striking position.

3. Apple's Shot on iPhone Mission: The client created content displaying the capacities of iPhone cameras and utilized the hashtag #ShotOniPhone to encourage users to share their own photographs.

4. The We Accept Campaign of Airbnb: a response to encourage acceptance and inclusion Included a sincere Super Bowl promotion supporting their obligation to variety.

5. Old Flavor's The Man Your Man Could Smell Like Mission: A clever and essential mission, including a charming representative. Effectively rebranded Old Zest and circulated around the web via virtual entertainment.

6. ALS Ice Pail Challenge: a social media challenge that went viral to raise money and awareness for ALS. Urged individuals to dump cans of ice water on themselves, creating a far-reaching investment.

7. Pigeon's Genuine Magnificence Mission: Celebrating different magnificence and testing excellence guidelines. Used strong visuals and informing to resound with an expansive crowd.

8. Burger Lord's Doozy Diversion: Utilized geofencing to offer limited Beasts when clients were close to McDonald's. Inventive utilization of innovation and a perky way to deal with rivalry.

9. Spotify's Wrapped Mission: Yearly customized playlists and insights for clients. Produced client commitment and virtual entertainment sharing during the Christmas season.

10. Campaign "Always' #LikeAGirl": Intending to challenge generalizations and rethink the expression "like a young lady." Enabled ladies and started conversations on orientation discernments.

11. Starbucks' Red Cup Contention: Social media buzz was generated by Starbucks' seasonal changes to its red cups. I connected with clients and made a yearly expectation for the Christmas season.

12. REI's #OptOutside Mission: Shut down stores on the biggest shopping day of the year, empowering clients to invest energy outside. Lined up with their image esteems and got positive acknowledgment.

13. Change at Domino's Pizza: They recognized deficiencies in their pizza and redid the recipe. Straightforward and fair, this mission prompted expanded deals and client trust.

14. Hotel owned by Taco Bell: Made a spring-up lodging experience themed around the brand. significant media coverage and buzz on social media.

15. Amazon's Alexa Loses Her Voice: a commercial for the Super Bowl in which celebrities speak for Alexa. Comical and paramount, displaying Alexa's mix into her day-to-day existence.

These missions exhibit a variety of effective promotion methodologies, from personalization and inclusivity to creative innovation. Remember that what works can change depending on the business, interest group, and current social setting.

Brainstorming Creative Ideas for Unique Holiday

Totally, conceptualizing one-of-a kind occasion crusades includes taking advantage of the merry soul while standing apart from the opposition. Here are a few imaginative plans to start motivation:

1. Gift-Wrapping Challenge: Customers should be encouraged to share their special gift-wrapping talents. Have an online entertainment challenge with prizes for the most innovative and merry wrapping.

2. Advanced Coming Schedule: Make a computerized appearance schedule with day-to-day shocks or limits. Draw in your crowd every day, paving the way for special times of the year.

3. Virtual Occasion Party Packs: Give virtual occasion party units to remote groups or families. Incorporate themed embellishments, games, and an aide for a remarkable virtual social occasion.

4. St. Nick's List of Things to Get Mission: Request that clients make and offer their vacation lists of things to get. Select a couple of wishes to satisfy as a token of appreciation.

5. Surprise Flash Mob: Sort out an unexpected occasion streak crowd and offer the video on the web. Highlight representatives or even clients participating in the merry dance.

6. Do-It-Yourself Enhancement Instructional exercises: Share Do-It-Yourself occasion beautification instructional exercises via web-based entertainment. Urge clients to make their own merry style and offer the outcomes.

7. 12 Days of Giveaways: Run a "12 Days of Giveaways" crusade with day-to-day prizes. Keep clients invigorated and connected all through the Christmas season.

8. Good cause Cooperation: For a collaboration with a holiday theme, collaborate with a local charity. Make a charity event or donate a portion of holiday sales.

9. Virtual Ditty Chime in: Have a virtual hymn chime on occasion via web-based entertainment. Urge devotees to share their interpretations for an opportunity to win prizes.

10. Boxes of Unknown Gifts: Provide surprise holiday gift boxes that are a mystery. Create a feeling of energy and expectation for clients.

11. Intuitive Narrating: Foster an intuitive occasion story on your site or through virtual entertainment. Permit clients to add to the story's movement.

12. Holiday Cards with Personalization: Give adjustable advanced occasion cards to clients to customize. Share the most innovative ones on your web-based entertainment stages.

13. Snow Globe Photograph Challenge: Urge clients to make their own snow globes. Run a photograph challenge displaying their remarkable snow globe plans.

14. Virtual St. Nick Meet-and-Welcome: Have a virtual St. Nick meet-and-welcome for families. Allow children to send Santa online their holiday wishes.

15. Bubbly Recipe Trade: Work with a bubbly recipe trade among clients. Share the most well-known recipes on your site or through virtual entertainment.

16. Winter Wonderland Forager Chase: Make a virtual or actual winter wonderland forager chase. Draw in members with difficulties and occasion-themed signs.

17. Merry Pet Procession: Urge clients to share photographs of their pets in occasion clothing. On your social media accounts, feature the most joyful pets.

18. Occasion Film Long-distance race: Have a virtual occasion to film a long-distance race with a live visit. Share suggestions and random data all through the long-distance race.

19. Bubbly Virtual Foundation Challenge: Challenge customers to design the most festive background for a virtual meeting. Grant prizes for inventiveness and occasion.

20. New Year, New Objectives Mission: Encourage customers to share their resolutions for the new year. Offer limits or motivations to help their objectives.

Always remember to adapt these concepts to your brand's personality, audience, and marketing goals. During the holiday season, the objective is to create experiences that customers will remember and find interesting.

Integrating User-Generated Content for Authenticity

Coordinating client-produced content (UGC) into your showcasing system can add genuineness and commitment. This is the way you can really integrate UGC:

1. Web-based Entertainment Hashtag Missions: Make a marked hashtag for clients to label their substance. Curate and offer the best UGC on your virtual entertainment stages.

2. Testimonials and Reviews from Clients: Highlight client surveys and tributes on your site. Exhibit genuine encounters to construct trust and validity.

3. Item Grandstands: Urge clients to share photographs or recordings including your items. Share these features on your site, virtual entertainment, or item pages.

4. Challenges and Contests: Have UGC challenges or difficulties with explicit subjects? Reward members with prizes and feature their entrances.

5. In the background Content: Demand clients share in the background looks at utilizing your items or administrations. Refine your image and give a veritable glance at the client experience.

6. Request Input and Ideas: Urge clients to give criticism or propose enhancements. Demonstrate that customer feedback is important by sharing the feedback loop.

7. Producing Content Together: Create joint content by working with customers or influencers. Exhibiting organizations improves genuineness and extends your range.

8. Feature Client Stories: Highlight individual stories or excursions of your clients. Make blog entries, web-based entertainment features, or video series around these accounts.

9. UGC Exhibitions on Site: Make a committed UGC exhibition on your site. Feature an assortment of content that mirrors the variety of your client base.

10. Live back and forth. Discussions: Conduct live Q&A sessions with questions from customers. Address concerns and connect straightforwardly with your crowd.

11. Client Takeovers: Permit clients to assume control over your online entertainment represents a day. Gives a credible perspective on your image from their perspective.

12. Videos of Testimonials: Demand clients to make video tributes. Video tributes add an individual touch and legitimacy.

13. Local area discussions: Lay out local area discussions for clients to interface with. Cultivate conversations and permit clients to naturally share encounters.

14. Faithfulness Projects: Integrate UGC into faithfulness programs. Reward clients for sharing their encounters and being brand advocates.

15. Recommendations for Personalized Products: Inquire from your clients about their favorite products and how they use them. Make personalized product recommendations using this UGC.

16. Client-Created Audits on Promotions: Highlight pieces of client-created audits in your publicizing. By displaying authentic testimonials, you can increase trust.

17. Partnerships with Influencers: Band together with powerhouses who really use and love your items. Their substance can act as UGC and bona fide supports.

18. Highlights of Employees: Exhibit UGC, highlighting your representatives utilizing or discussing your items. Refine your image by highlighting the individuals behind it.

19. Surveys and polls: Customer feedback can be gathered through surveys and polls. Share the outcomes and exhibit that client input shapes your image.

20. Observe Achievements Together: Celebrate brand achievements by empowering clients to share how they've been essential for your excursion. Encourage a sense of local area and shared achievement.

By coordinating UGC truly, you not just interface with your crowd on an individual level yet in addition make a feeling of local area around your image. Screen and draw in with UGC consistently to keep a continuous, unique relationship with your clients.

Chapter 8: Customer Retention Strategies

Client maintenance is indispensable for the drawn-out progress of any business. The following are successful methods for increasing customer retention:

1. Customized Correspondence: Tailor your correspondence in view of client inclinations and ways of behaving. Utilize customized messages and offers to cause clients to feel esteemed.

2. Faithfulness Projects: Carry out dedication programs with remunerations, limits, or selective advantages. Boost rehash buys and encourage client steadfastness.

3. Outstanding client support: Offer helpful and prompt customer service. Work quickly to solve problems, and go above and beyond to meet or exceed the needs of your customers.

4. Ordinary Commitment: Remain in touch with your clients through standard updates. Share applicable substances,

advancements, and news to keep up with top-of-mind mindfulness.

5. Client Input and Studies: Accumulate input to grasp consumer loyalty. Surveys can be used to address concerns and pinpoint areas for improvement.

6. Access or exclusive content: Offer restrictive substance, early access, or sneak looks to faithful clients. Make a sense of selectiveness to fortify the client-brand relationship.

7. Repeating Charging or Membership Models: Use services that require a subscription or recurring payments. Give accommodation to clients while guaranteeing unsurprising income for your business.

8. Commemoration and Achievement Festivities: Celebrate client commemorations or achievements. Send customized messages or offers to celebrate their excursion with your image.

9. Virtual Entertainment Commitment: Engage customers on social media actively. Participate in discussions, respond to comments, and share user-generated content.

10. Proactive Issue Goal: Expect likely issues and address them proactively. Exhibit a promise to consumer loyalty by settling issues before they arise.

11. Gamification: Acquaint gamification components with support for client commitment. To make interactions enjoyable, incorporate point systems, challenges, or rewards.

12. Persistent Worth Expansion: Consistently increase the value of your items or services. Keep customers engaged by introducing new features, updates, or complementary offerings.

13. Surprise and Satisfaction: Infrequently shock clients with surprising gifts, limits, or selective offers. Make essential minutes to cultivate positive feelings.

14. Client Instruction and Preparing: Help customers make the most of the products they buy by offering resources or training. Give them the authority to make the most of your services.

15. Social Verification and Tributes: Exhibit positive surveys, tributes, and examples of overcoming adversity. Fabricate trust and believability, impacting other potential clients decisively.

16. Client People Group: Lay out internet-based discussions or networks for your clients. Encourage peer-to-peer support, shared experiences, and interaction.

17. Multi-Channel Presence: Be available across various channels for consistent client communication. Guarantee consistency in information and administration quality.

18. Customized Proposals: Use information to give customized item proposals. Improve the client shopping experience with custom-made ideas.

19. Forthcoming Restoration Updates: In the event that is appropriate, send updates for impending reestablishments or repurchases. Give impetus to support opportune restorations.

20. Continual Development: Routinely evaluate client input and adjust your techniques. Exhibit a guarantee to develop in view of client needs.

You will not only be able to keep the customers you already have by concentrating on these tactics, but you will also be able to build relationships that last a lifetime and will contribute to the expansion and success of your business. Reliable endeavors to comprehend, draw in, and enhance your client base will deliver profits over the long haul.

Loyalty Programs and Exclusive Offers

Carrying out unwaveringly projects and elite offers can essentially improve client maintenance. This is the way you can really plan and execute them:

Devotion   Projects:
1. Focuses-Based Frameworks: Grant focuses for each buy, which clients can reclaim for limits, items, or restrictive encounters.
2. Programs with tiers of loyalty: Make levels with expanding benefits in light of client unwaveringness. Higher levels can offer restrictive advantages, like early access to deals or customized   help.
3. Birthday Gifts: Send customized birthday offers or presents to celebrate clients. This adds an individual touch and encourages a positive   close-to-home   association.
4. Reference Prizes: Utilize referral programs to encourage customers to refer family and friends. Offer limits, free items, or focuses   for   fruitful   references.
5. Select Occasions: Have occasions only for faithful clients, either face-to-face or virtually. Give early admittance to new items, extraordinary limits, or in-the-background encounters.
6. Membership Models: Present membership-based dependability programs. Clients pay a repetitive expense for premium advantages such as free transportation or restrictive substances.
7. Gamification: Integrate gamification components into unwaveringness programs. Make difficulties, journeys, or rivalries   to   keep   clients   locked   in.
8. Commemoration Prizes: On the anniversary of a customer's membership, recognize and reward them. To commemorate the

occasion, provide exclusive deals or discounts.
9. Spend-Based Prizes: Reward clients in light of their complete investment in energy. Give heightening advantages to arriving at explicit burning through achievements.
10. Discounts tailored to you: Offer customized limits in light of individual inclinations and buy history. Tailor offers to line up with every client's advantages.
Select Offers:
1. Early Access Deals: Give faithful clients early access to deals or new item dispatches. A sense of exclusivity and appreciation are created as a result.
2. Restricted Time Advancements: For a limited time, provide exclusive discounts or promotions. Make earnestness drive prompt commitment.
3. Celebrity Participations: Introduce a VIP membership with exclusive advantages. This can incorporate selective items, need support, or customized administrations.
4. Individuals Just Satisfied: Share individuals just satisfied, for example, blog entries, recordings, or articles. Keep clients drawn in with important and restrictive data.
5. Tweaked Groups: Make selective item packages or bundles for steadfast clients. Offer these packs at a limited cost or with extra advantages.
6. Trials or Free Samples: Furnish faithful clients with free examples or preliminary adaptations of new items. This permits them to encounter new contributions before the overall crowd.
7. Twofold Focuses or Rewards Days: Designate specific days on which customers can receive rewards or double points. Empower expanded cooperation during these limited time periods.
8. Cooperation with Partners: Team up with different brands for selective offers. Make one-of-a kind organizations that benefit both your image and your clients.
9. Select Admittance to Master Guidance: Offer steadfast clients

access to industry specialists or customized guidance. This adds value to past items and constructs a feeling of mastery. 10. Shock Prizes: Give gifts or rewards to loyal customers that you didn't expect. These unforeseen signals enhance the sensation of appreciation.

Make sure to advance faithfulness projects and elite proposals through different channels, including email bulletins, web-based entertainment, and on your site. Routinely impart the value clients get as a feature of these projects to keep them connected with and spurred to remain faithful to your image.

Personalized Recommendations and Retargeting

Personalized recommendations and retargeting are potent methods for engaging customers and boosting conversion rates. This is the way you can really execute them:

Personalize Recommendations:

1. Conduct-Based Proposals: Break down client perusal and buy history to propose items in view of their inclinations and conduct.

2. Cooperative Sifting: Collaborative filtering algorithms can be used to make product recommendations based on similar customer preferences.

3. Item Packages: Suggest item packages or reciprocal things in view of clients' past purchases. This empowers upselling and improves the shopping experience.

4. A list of things to get Updates: Help clients remember things on their lists of things to get.

To encourage conversions, provide individualized incentives such as discounts or exclusive access.

5. Occasional Proposals: Tailor proposals to line up with occasional patterns and client inclinations. Exhibit items pertinent to occasions, climates, or occasions.

6. Dynamic Substance on Site: Customize the substance shown on your site in view of client inclinations. On the homepage, display items or suggestions that have been viewed recently.

7. Customized Email Missions: Personalized email campaigns can be created by making use of customer data. Send targeted emails with product recommendations or special offers.

8. Computer-based intelligence Fueled Suggestions: Carry out man-made reasoning to investigate huge datasets and give more precise and dynamic suggestions.

9. Geo-Designated Suggestions: Think about recommendations based on where you are. Propose items or administrations in light of the client's area or neighborhood patterns.

10. Inclination Focuses: Permit clients to set inclinations through inclination habitats. Make use of this data to improve and refine individual recommendations.

Retargeting:

1. Deserted Truck Retargeting: Remind clients about things left in their shopping baskets through designated advertisements. Incorporate motivating forces like limits to energize the finish of the buy.

2. Dynamic Retargeting Promotions: Utilize dynamic promotions that highlight items a client saw or showed interest in. This gives a customized and outwardly engaging update.

3. Strategically pitch and upsell Retargeting: Based on their previous purchases, retarget customers with complementary or upgraded products. Urge them to investigate extra choices.

4. Post-Buy Retargeting: Show promotions for related items after a client makes a buy. This keeps them connected with and energizes rehash business.

5. Time-Delicate Offers: Make desperation with time-delicate retargeting offers. Feature restricted time limits or selective arrangements to provoke activity.

6. Campaigns for Segmented Retargeting: Portion your crowd in light of their associations with your site. Convey customized retargeting messages in view of explicit ways of behaving.

7. Tweaked Points of Arrival: Direct retargeting traffic to altered points of arrival. Guarantee the page content lines up with the items or content they recently drew in with.

8. Client Excursion Retargeting: Adjust retargeting endeavors with the client's excursion. Tailor messages in view of where they are in the deal pipe.

9. Retargeting on social media: Execute retargeting promotions via virtual entertainment stages. When customers are active on social media, remind them of the products they saw on your website.

10. Criticism and Survey Solicitations: Retarget clients with demands for input or audits. Utilize this as a potential chance to

upgrade consumer loyalty and accumulate significant experiences.

Consolidate customized suggestions with retargeting endeavors to make a consistent and drawing-in experience for your clients. Persistently examine information and client cooperation to refine your methodologies and adjust to advancing inclinations.

Post-Purchase Engagement for Repeat Business

Post-buy commitment is urgent for building enduring client connections and empowering rehash business. Here are successful procedures to keep clients connected after their underlying purchase:

1. Request confirmation and much obliged: Immediately following the purchase, send a personalized order confirmation and thank-you email. Offer thanks and affirm the subtleties of the exchange.

2. Surveys after the purchase: Assemble criticism through post-purchase studies. Figure out the client's insight and use bits of knowledge for upgrades.

3. Dedication Program Presentation: Acquaint clients with your faithfulness program. Feature the advantages and rewards they can acquire through recurrent purchases.

4. Special Offers for Your Next Purchase: Remember restrictive limits or offers for the post-purchase correspondence. Urge clients to return for their next buy.

5. Important Item Proposals: Give customized item proposals in light of their new purchase. Propose corresponding things or adornments they may be keen on.

6. Virtual Entertainment Commitment: Urge clients to share their purchases via web-based entertainment. Make a sense of the local area and appreciate their involvement in your image.

7. Instructive Substance: Share an instructive substance connected with the bought item. Tips, tutorials, or user guides can help them learn and use the software better.

8. Membership Updates: Remind customers about subscription refills or renewals, if necessary. Make the cycle consistent and advantageous.

9. Personalized Cards of Appreciation: Include a customized card of appreciation in the package. Special touches or notes written by hand add a personal touch.

10. Strategically pitch Suggestions: Suggest items that supplement their underlying purchase. Feature how these increments can improve their general insight.

11. Follow-Up Email Series: Execute a subsequent email series to monitor consumer loyalty. Continuously present extra items or advantages they may be keen on.

12. Anniversary Offers for Customers: Commend the commemoration of their most memorable buy with extraordinary offers. Make their connection to your brand stronger.

13. Celebrity Client Status: Recognize Rehash clients as celebrities. Offer select advantages, early access to deals, or customized administrations.

14. Gamified Commitment: Acquaint gamification components with keeping clients locked in. Reward repeats customers with badges, challenges, or points.

15. Demand Item Audits: Urge clients to leave surveys for the bought item. Offer motivators or take part in a survey challenge.

16. Occasion Solicitations: Customers can be invited to exclusive events in person or online. Cause them to feel part of a unique local area.

17. Customized Email Missions: Use information from their most memorable buy to make customized email crusades. Suggest fresh introductions or restricted-time advancements in light of their inclinations.

18. Local area cooperation: support cooperation in local area gatherings or conversations. Connect customers who have similar interests by making connections easier.

19. Instructive Online classes or studios: Have online courses or studios connected with the item or industry. Position your image as a power and offer some benefit beyond the buy.

20. Bother Free Returns and Trades: Convey an issue-free return or trade process. Guarantee clients have good expectations about their buying choices.

Predictable and insightful post-purchase commitment shows your obligation to consumer loyalty and lays the groundwork for an enduring relationship. Tailor your methodology in view of your industry, item contributions, and the inclinations of your client

Data analytics and measurement

Information investigation and estimation are fundamental parts of grasping the presentation of your business, enhancing systems, and settling on informed choices. Here is an exhaustive guide to utilizing information examination and estimation successfully:

1. Characterize clear goals: Clearly characterize your business goals and key execution pointers (KPIs). Adjust information examination endeavors with your all-encompassing objectives.

2. Pick Pertinent Measurements: Select measurements that straightforwardly line up with your goals. Stay away from vanity measurements and shine a spotlight on those that provide noteworthy experiences.

3. Carry out Information Assortment Apparatuses: Set up powerful information assortment devices, like Google Investigation, for online stages. Integrate your app, website, or other relevant platforms correctly.

4. Client Excursion Planning: Map the client excursion to comprehend touchpoints and associations. Recognize key minutes that add to changes or client fulfillment.

5. Use A/B Testing: Conduct A/B testing for product variations, marketing campaigns, or elements of the website. Dissect results to pursue information-driven choices on what works best.

6. Client Division: Portion your crowd in view of socioeconomics, conduct, or other significant variables. Tailor promotion procedures for each fragment to improve personalization.

7. Analytics for social media: Make use of social media platform analytics tools. Understand the impact of social media efforts and monitor engagement.

8. Execution Advertising Examination: Investigate the exhibition of paid promotional efforts. Assess the profit from speculation

(return on initial capital investment) for various channels and change financial plans as needed.

9. Change Rate Advancement (CRO): Carry out CRO systems to work on the proficiency of your change channel. Distinguish and address boundaries to transformation in view of information experiences.

10. Prescient Examination: Investigate prescient examination to gauge future patterns. Patterns and proactive decisions can be identified using machine-learning algorithms.

11. Continuous Examination: Execute constant investigation for sure fire experiences. Be quick to respond to new trends or problems that affect your business.

12. Information Perception: Use information perception instruments to make clear, reasonable portrayals of information. Dashboards and charts can speed up the decision-making process.

13. Analysis of a Cohort: Lead a companion investigation to track and think about gatherings of clients over the long run. Comprehend client ways of behaving and distinguish regions for development.

14. Site Execution Measurements: Keep an eye on the performance metrics of your website, such as page load times and bounce rates. Upgrade for a consistent client experience.

15. Portable Investigation: Investigate information intended for versatile clients. Guarantee your advanced procedures are enhanced for versatile stages.

16. Information Security Consistence: Focus on information protection and guarantee consistency with significant guidelines. Build trust by handling and storing customer data securely.

17. Continual Development: Consistently audit and refine your information examination methodology. Adapt to shifting consumer preferences and market conditions.

18. Information-Driven Culture: Encourage an information-driven culture inside your association. Urge groups to put together choices with respect to information and experiences instead of suspicions.

19. Attribution Displaying: Carry out attribution models to comprehend the commitment of each showcasing channel. Dispense assets in light of the channels that drive the most worth.

20. Screen Contender Measurements: Watch out for the measurements and techniques of your rivals. Assess the market for opportunities and threats.

Powerful information examination and estimation enable your business to remain light, pursue informed choices, and ceaselessly move along. Routinely rethink your examination procedure to remain in line with your business objectives and developing business sector elements.

Implementing Analytics Tools for Campaign Tracking

Executing investigation devices for crusade following is essential for estimating the achievement and effect of your advertising endeavors. Here is a bit-by-bit manual to assist you with successfully setting up investigation devices:

1. Recognize Key Measurements: Choose the campaign's key performance indicators (KPIs). These could incorporate change rates, navigation rates, commitment measurements, and so on.

2. Pick Examination Instruments: Select investigation instruments that line up with your mission objectives. Google Analytics, Adobe Analytics, and social media analytics platforms are all common instruments.

3. Set Up Google Examination: In the case of utilizing Google Examination, make a record and set up a property for your site. Introduce the following code on your site to begin gathering information.

4. Characterize mission URLs: Use UTM boundaries to make custom mission URLs. This helps track the source, medium, and explicit mission subtleties in examination apparatuses.

5. Incorporate with Promoting Stages: Ads platforms like Google Ads and Facebook Ads should be integrated with analytics tools. To monitor ad performance in your analytics dashboard, check for proper linking.

6. Lay out objectives and changes: Characterize objectives inside your examination device to quantify explicit activities (e.g., structure entries, buys). Set up a web-based business, if pertinent.

7. Occasion Following: Execute occasion following for cooperations not caught naturally (e.g., video sees, button clicks). This gives a more itemized comprehension of client commitment.

8. Online Entertainment Examination Mix: Integrate social media platforms with your analytics tool. This empowers the following of online entertainment crusade execution inside your investigation dashboard.

9. Attribution Models: Pick an attribution model that lines up with your business objectives. Break down how different touchpoints contribute to changes.

10. Custom Dashboards: Make custom dashboards inside your examination device. Orchestrate gadgets to show the most important mission measurements initially.

11. Keep a regular eye on the data: Routinely screen your examination dashboard for ongoing bits of knowledge. Recognize patterns, oddities, or regions that need improvement.

12. The A/B Test: Set up A/B tests for various campaign components. Use investigation to think about the presentation of varieties and refine your system.

13. Information Quality Checks: Guarantee information precision by performing normal information quality checks. Check that the following codes are accurately executed and that the information lines up with assumptions.

14. Regular Reports: Create occasional reports summarizing crusade execution. Share bits of knowledge with pertinent partners to illuminate independent direction.

15. Segmentation of Users: Use client divisions to investigate explicit crowd gatherings. Comprehend how various sections connect with your mission.

16. Portable Examination Arrangement: Assuming your mission targets portable clients, set up a versatile examination. Break down portable explicit measurements and client conduct.

17. Client Excursion Examination: Dissect the client venture inside your investigation apparatus. Recognize well-known ways, sections, and endless points of drop-off.

18. Information Security Consistence: Make sure that data privacy laws are followed. Carry out highlights like IP anonymization in Google Examination to safeguard client security.

19. Ceaseless Advancement: Use investigational bits of knowledge for persistent enhancement. Change crusade components in view of information-driven ends.

20. Documentation and instruction: Give preparation to colleagues on utilizing investigation instruments. Report cycles and best practices to keep up with consistency.

You can build a solid analytics framework for monitoring and evaluating your campaigns' success by following these steps. Adjust your analytics strategy on a regular basis to keep up with shifting campaign goals and market dynamics.

Analyzing Key Metrics and KPIs

Investigating key measurements and key execution pointers (KPIs) is fundamental for assessing the progress of your business or mission. Here is a manual to assist you with really examining these measurements:

1. Characterize key measurements: Distinguish the particular measurements pertinent to your objectives. Normal

measurements incorporate change rates, navigate rates, bob rates, income, and client procurement costs.

2. Grasp Your Targets: Adjust measurements to your business or mission goals. Obviously, characterize what achievement resembles for your association.

3. Zero in on KPIs: Focus on key execution markers (KPIs) that straightforwardly influence your main concern. KPIs could incorporate income development, client lifetime worth, or profit from ventures (return for capital invested).

4. Intermittent Execution Audits: Direct normal surveys of your key measurements. Monitor performance over time to discover patterns, trends, or weak spots.

5. Benchmarking: Examine your metrics in relation to industry norms. Comprehend how your presentation has what it takes in your area.

6. Change Pipe Investigation: Break down each phase of your change pipe. Recognize possible drop-off focuses and enhance in like manner.

7. Client Division: Divide metrics into segments of customers. Comprehend how different client bunches contribute to general execution.

8. Attribution Displaying: Execute attribution models to assign worth to different touchpoints. Comprehend the client venture and apportion credit appropriately.

9. Analysis of a Cohort: Use companion examination to follow the way of behaving of explicit gatherings over the long run. Examine how various companions contribute to general speaking execution.

10. Client Maintenance Measurements: Dissect client maintenance measurements like stir rate and rehash buy rate. Figure out the drawn-out worth of your client connections.

11. Cost Measurements: Assess cost measurements, for example, client procurement cost (CAC) and advertising spend. Guarantee that your expenses line up with the value produced.

12. Client Commitment Measurements: Analyze client commitment measurements like time nearby, site hits, and social offers. Understand how drawn in your crowd is by your substance or stage.

13. Insightful Apparatuses: Make use of analytics tools to make data analysis easier. Apparatuses like Google Investigation, Mix panel, or Adobe Examination give important bits of knowledge.

14. Continuous Monitoring: Carry out constant checking of key measurements. Respond quickly to any unexpected changes or issues influencing execution.

15. Set Edges and Alarms: Set thresholds for important metrics. Set up alarms to inform you when measurements go amiss from anticipated values.

16. Heatmaps and Client Conduct Examination: To learn how users interact with your website or app, use heatmaps and user behavior analysis. Find out where people are most and least engaged.

17. Information Perception: Use information perception strategies. Interpreting intricate data is made simpler by dashboards, graphs, and charts.

18. A/B Testing Investigation: Dissect results from A/B testing. Recognize varieties that lead to further execution and carry out those changes.

19. Continual Development: Lay out a culture of constant improvement. Metrics can help you iterate and improve your strategies.

20. Share Bits of Knowledge Across Groups: Convey experiences across important groups. Cultivate cooperation and adjust endeavors in view of shared information-driven ends.

A viable examination of key measurements and KPIs gives an establishment to informed direction, permitting you to streamline systems, dispense assets really, and drive generally business achievement. Keep revisiting and refining your strategy on a regular basis as your company grows.

Iterative Optimization Based on Data Insights

Iterative streamlining in light of information bits of knowledge is a ceaseless and versatile cycle that includes refining techniques, missions, and client encounters in view of the examination of information. This is an aid while heading to iteratively streamline utilizing information bits of knowledge:

1. Lay out an information-driven culture: Encourage a culture inside your association that values information-driven direction. Urge groups to depend on informational experiences to direct their activities.

2. Persistent Checking: Carry out persistent observing of key measurements and KPIs. Consistently survey information to distinguish examples, patterns, or peculiarities.

3. A/B testing and trial and error: Direct A/B tests and investigations to look at varieties. Use information to figure out which varieties yield improved results and emphasize them appropriately.

4. Integration of User Feedback: Include feedback from customers in the optimization process. Consider criticism from client assistance, studies, and online entertainment to upgrade systems.

5. Responsive Procedure Change: Be receptive to changes in information patterns. Change systems quickly founded on shifts in client conduct or economic situations.

6. Use heatmaps and client examination: Break down heatmaps and have the client conduct an investigation. Distinguish areas of high and low commitment and make adjustments to further develop client encounters.

7. Iterative Site and Application Enhancement: Keep improving your app or website based on how users interact with it. Test and refine components like routes, designs, and CTAs.

8. Personalization Procedures: Execute personalization procedures in view of client inclinations and conduct. Tailor content, proposals, and advertising messages to individual client needs.

9. Client Excursion Examination: Break down the client venture from attention to transformation. Recognize grating focuses and enhance the excursion for a smoother client experience.

10. Spry Showcasing Procedures: Take on coordinated promotion methods that consider fast cycles. Divide projects into smaller, more manageable tasks, and make adjustments in response to regular feedback.

11. Occasional Technique Surveys: Lead intermittent audits of general techniques. Evaluate the viability of missions, channels, and information.

12. AI and Prescient Investigation: Carry out AI and prescient examinations for cutting-edge experiences. Expect future patterns and proactively change methodologies.

13. Information Representation for Correspondence: Utilize tools for data visualization to effectively convey insights. Make dashboards or reports that convey complex information in an edible configuration.

14. Cross-Useful Cooperation: Cultivate coordinated efforts between various groups. Separate storehouses and urge cross-useful conversations to share experiences.

15. Cutthroat Examination: Break down the procedures of contenders. Distinguish regions where your association can separate or further develop in view of market patterns.

16. Regular instruction and development of skills: Put resources into ordinary preparation for your group on the most recent apparatuses and procedures. To be able to analyze data effectively, keep skills current.

17. Enhancement of the Customer Persona: Refine client personas in view of advancing information. Guarantee that promoting messages and procedures line up with the changing requirements of your crowd.

18. Optimization of the Technology Stack: Routinely survey and improve your innovation stack. Guarantee that the devices you use are lined up with your developing business needs.

19. Strategies for Retaining Users: Ceaselessly refine client maintenance systems. Find and implement strategies that keep current clients engaged and committed.

20. Information Protection and Consistency: Keep up to date with information security guidelines and consistency. Guarantee that streamlining endeavors line up with lawful and moral principles.

The process of iterative optimization is always changing. You can adapt your strategies to meet changing user expectations and market demands by adopting a mindset of continuous improvement and remaining responsive to data insights. Routinely reevaluate and refine your improvement methods to stay ahead in a powerful business scene.

Conclusion

All in all, utilizing computerized showcasing systems for Christmas season achievement is a dynamic and fundamental undertaking for organizations meaning to benefit from the bubbly season. The joining of information-driven experiences, exhaustive preparation, and a multichannel approach is fundamental to coming to and resounding with the occasion crowd. By embracing the force of advanced showcasing instruments, organizations can expand their perceivability as well as make connections and customized encounters that encourage client dependability.

Key Procedures for Occasional Achievement

1. Early Preparation: Start holiday planning far in advance to ensure that promotions and campaigns run smoothly.

2. Grasping Crowd: Acquire profound experiences into your ideal interest group's way of behaving, inclinations, and buying designs during the Christmas season.

3. Multichannel Approach: Execute a multichannel showcasing procedure that incorporates web-based entertainment, email promotion, content promotion, and paid publicizing.

4. Personalization: Use information to customize showcasing messages and offers, making a more significant association with clients.

5. Portable Streamlining: Recognizing the growing trend of mobile holiday shopping, optimize all digital assets for mobile devices.

6. Strategic Sales and Discounts: Mindfully configure limits and advancements to draw in clients while keeping up with productivity.

7. Email Showcasing Greatness: Influence the force of email advertising with drawing-in and customized crusades, including select occasion offers.

8. Virtual Entertainment Commitment: Amplify online entertainment commitment by making shareable substance, running occasion-themed challenges, and utilizing forces to be reckoned with.

9. Site design improvement (website optimization): Improve site happiness with occasion-themed catchphrases to upgrade perceivability in web crawler results.

10. Client Maintenance Procedures: To keep current customers interested, implement customer retention strategies like a loyalty program.

11. Information Investigation and Estimation: Utilize strong investigation apparatuses to gauge the presentation of occasion crusades and determine significant experiences for advancement.

12. Persistent Iterative Advancement: Constantly emphasize and streamline techniques in view of continuous information and experiences, adjusting to changing business sector elements.

13. Client-Produced Content: To build authenticity and encourage customers to share their holiday experiences with your brand, incorporate user-generated content.

14. Versatile Promoting Best Practices: Execute best practices for versatile advertising, taking into account the commonness of cell phone use during the Christmas season.

15. Client Excursion Examination: Investigate the client venture during special times of year to distinguish touchpoints and regions for development.

16. Serious Investigation: Remain informed about the techniques utilized by contenders, permitting your business to separate and remain serious.

17. Social Business Elements: Influence social trade highlights on stages like Instagram and Facebook to work with consistent shopping encounters.

18. Email Groupings for Client Maintenance: Advance email successions to support client connections post-buy, empowering rehash business.

19. Vital Associations: Investigate key associations with different organizations or powerhouses to extend your span and improve validity.

Dexterous Advertising Methods: Embrace deft showcasing strategies for speedy variation in developing patterns and client assumptions.

By decisively integrating these key techniques, organizations can explore the Christmas season effectively, expanding their scope, commitment, and transformations during this significant season.

Recap of Key Strategies for Holiday Success

The following are a few key strategies for a successful holiday season:

1. Arranging and Planning: Make a thorough plan for the holiday season early on. Recognize your objectives, interest group, and key special periods. Create a comprehensive schedule and budget for staffing, inventory, and marketing.

2. Client-Driven Approach: Center around conveying extraordinary client encounters. Train your staff to offer customized and mindful support, offer clear and opportune correspondence, and address client requests instantly. Consider executing reliability projects or restrictive proposals to compensate and hold steadfast clients.

3. Stock and store network The board: To accurately forecast demand, examine historical sales data and market trends. Guarantee you have adequate stock to address client issues; however, abstain from overloading to limit stock holding costs. Lay areas of strength with providers and enhance your inventory network to decrease conveyance lead times.

Emphasizing the Long-Term Benefits of Effective Digital Marketing

It is essential for businesses that want to continue growing and succeeding in the long run to put an emphasis on the long-term benefits of digital marketing. Here is an emphasis on the getting-through benefits that result from a professional computerized showcasing system:

- Brand Building and Acknowledgment: Develop brand recognition over time and establish a robust online presence. Predictable computerized advertising endeavors add to trust and devotion.
- Client Relationship Building: Fashion significant associations with clients through customized and designated correspondence. Sustain long-haul client unwaveringness and support.

- Information-Driven Navigation: Ceaselessly accumulate and break down information to illuminate vital choices. Upgrade the proficiency of promoting endeavors by adjusting in view of experiences.

- Worldwide Reach and Availability: Extend your reach beyond past topographical limits through web-based channels. Access a worldwide crowd and differentiate your client base.

- Lead Age and Change: Continuously generate leads through digital marketing channels. Establish a consistent flow of potential customers who can be converted over time.

- Continuously changing with the times: Remain in front of industry patterns and purchaser's ways of behaving. Adjust advertising methodologies to line up with changing business sector elements.

- Savvy Promoting: Influence financially savvy computerized promoting channels for productive effort. Achieve an exceptional yield on speculation compared with customary showcasing strategies.

- Authority and Thought Initiative: Your company should establish itself as an authority in its field. Position yourself as an idea chief through important substance and skill.

- Spryness in Showcasing Methodologies: Immediately adjust to showcase changes and purchaser inclinations. Carry out light-footed showcasing procedures for responsiveness.

- Local area commitment: Encourage a feeling of local area around your image.

Draw in clients via virtual entertainment and different stages to create a devoted local area.

By featuring these getting-through benefits, organizations can highlight the worth of a vital and long-term way to deal with computerized showcasing. The combined effect of predictable endeavors in the computerized space contributes fundamentally to supported development and flexibility in a serious market.

Encouragement for Businesses to Adapt and Innovate

Empowering organizations to adjust and advance is fundamental to remaining important and cutting-edge in the present unique scene. Here are a few inspirational focuses to move organizations to embrace change:

1. Embrace a Development Mentality: Develop a mentality that views challenges as any open doors for development. Embrace change with excitement, considering it to be an opportunity to develop.

2. Remain Deft and Responsive: Be nimble in answering business sector patterns and shopper needs. Readiness considers speedy changes and positions your business as receptive to change.

3. Champion a Culture of Development: Cultivate a hierarchical culture that values and prizes development. Urge representatives to contribute their thoughts and go ahead with reasonable courses of action.

4. Learn from Mistakes: View disappointment as a venturing stone toward progress. Gain from mistakes, emphasize, and use

disappointments as important examples in the advancement cycle.

5. Utilize New Technologies: Embrace new innovations that can alter your industry. Remain informed about emerging patterns and be an early adopter where it seems OK.

6. Client-Driven Approach: Focus on a client-driven approach in your business systems. Advance in light of client criticism and developing inclinations.

7. Joint efforts and associations: Look for coordinated efforts and associations with different organizations. Joint endeavors and associations can bring new points of view and shared assets.

8. Put resources into Representative Turn of events: Put resources into the ceaseless improvement of your labor force. Thoroughly prepared and talented workers are better prepared to contribute to development.

9. Stir things up: Your team should be encouraged to question assumptions and the status quo. Advancement frequently comes from splitting away from regular reasoning.

10. Make a Culture of Ceaseless Learning: Advance ceaseless advancement at all levels of the association. Outfit your group with the information and abilities required for progressing development.

Empowering organizations to adjust and advance isn't just about endurance; it's tied in with flourishing in a quickly developing world. By cultivating a culture that values imagination, embraces change, and focuses on constant improvement, organizations can situate themselves for supported outcomes over the long haul.